IT Governance

Implementing Frameworks and Standards for the Corporate Governance of IT

IT Governance

Implementing Frameworks and Standards for the Corporate Governance of IT

**ALAN CALDER
WITH
STEVE MOIR**

IT Governance Publishing

IT Governance Publishing
IT Governance Limited
Unit 3, Clive Court
Bartholomew's Walk
Cambridgeshire Business Park
Ely
Cambridgeshire
CB7 4EH
United Kingdom

www.itgovernance.co.uk

First published in the United Kingdom in 2009
by IT Governance Publishing.

ISBN 978-1-905356-90-4

FOREWORD

Corporate governance increasingly provides the context within which twenty-first century organisations have to assess and deal with their investments in, and risks to, their corporate information assets and the Information and Communications Technology (ICT, or just IT) infrastructure within which those information assets are collected, manipulated, stored and deployed. But what is corporate governance, and why is it important to the IT professional? Why is IT governance important to the company director, and what do directors of companies – both quoted and unquoted – need to know?

This book aims to do two things.

The first is to set out for managers, executives and IT professionals the practical steps necessary to meet today's corporate and IT governance requirements.

The second is to provide practical guidance on how board executives and IT professionals can navigate and deploy to best corporate and commercial advantage the numerous IT management and IT governance frameworks and standards – particularly ISO/IEC 38500 – that have been published over the course of the last 10 years. Each of these standards and frameworks has a potentially valuable role to play in the organisation; the challenge lies in integrating them so that each can deliver what it was designed to do, and do this within the context of an overarching framework (a 'super framework', or 'meta-framework') that enables each organisation to design IT governance to meet its own needs. The Calder-Moir Framework (which is freely available to download from *www.itgovernance.co.uk/calder_moir.aspx*)

was developed specifically to help organisations manage and govern their IT operations more effectively, and to coordinate the sometimes wide range of overlapping and competing frameworks and standards. It also specifically supports implementation of ISO/IEC 38500, the new international standard for best practice IT governance.

PREFACE

This book assembles, restructures and stitches together a number of Alan Calder's recent articles on aspects of IT governance and is designed to provide a current guide to this subject. It also introduces and contextualises the Calder-Moir Framework, a meta-model for IT governance. This book provides an overview of this framework and some perspectives on its implementation.

This book should be read alongside Alan's two other books on this subject: *IT Governance: Guidelines for Directors*[1] and *IT Governance Today: a Practitioner's Handbook*[2]. Both of these books are available from *www.itgovernance.co.uk*.

This book also serves as an effective introduction to the contents of the *IT Governance Framework Toolkit*[3] and, along with the two books mentioned above, provides a comprehensive toolset for the IT governance professional.

---

[1] Alan Calder, *IT Governance: Guidelines for Directors* (ITGP, 2005). See *www.itgovernance.co.uk/products/19*.
[2] Alan Calder, *IT Governance Today: a Practitioner's Handbook* (ITGP, 2005). See *www.itgovernance.co.uk/products/18*.
[3] *www.itgovernance.co.uk/products/519*.

ABOUT THE AUTHOR

Alan Calder is a leading author on information security and IT governance issues. He is Chief Executive of IT Governance Limited, the one-stop-shop for books, tools, training and consultancy on governance, risk management and compliance. He is also Chairman of the Board of Directors of CEME, a public-private sector skills partnership.

Alan is an international authority on IT Governance and, with Steve Moir, originated the innovative Calder-Moir IT Governance Framework. He is also an international expert on ISO27001 (formerly BS7799), the international security standard, about which he wrote with colleague Steve Watkins the definitive compliance guide, *IT Governance: A Manager's Guide to Data Security and BS7799/ISO17799*. This work is based on his experience of leading the world's first successful implementation of BS7799 (with the fourth edition published in May 2008) and is the basis for the UK Open University's postgraduate course on information security.

Other books written by Alan include *The Case for ISO27001*, *ISO27001 – Nine Steps to Success*, *IT Governance: Guidelines for Directors*, *IT Governance Today: a Practitioner's Handbook* and *IT Regulatory Compliance in the UK*.

Alan is a frequent media commentator on information security and IT governance issues, and has contributed articles and expert comment to a wide range of trade, national and online news outlets.

About the Author

Alan was previously CEO of Wide Learning, a supplier of e-learning; of Focus Central London, a training and enterprise council; and of Business Link London City Partners, a government agency focused on helping growing businesses to develop. He was a member of the Information Age Competitiveness Working Group of the UK Government's Department for Trade & Industry, and was until recently a member of the DNV Certification Services Certification Committee, which certifies compliance with international standards including ISO27001.

ACKNOWLEDGEMENTS

While this book was written by Alan Calder, elements of it (including almost all the graphical representations) were contributed by Steve Moir who, with Alan Calder, originated the Calder-Moir IT Governance Framework. Steve Moir created the *IT Governance Framework Toolkit*, which provides significant and extensive support to organisations implementing IT governance using the Calder-Moir Framework and ISO38500. Some of Alan's material has also appeared elsewhere, albeit in a slightly different form.

CONTENTS

Contents

Contents

INTRODUCTION: CORPORATE GOVERNANCE CONTEXT

Corporate governance is a daily newspaper subject and, to one extent or another, all company directors – and the directors of public sector and quasi-autonomous governmental organisations (known in the UK as 'quangos') – want to know what corporate governance really means for them. What is good corporate governance practice? To whom does the UK's Combined Code really apply? Is SOX[4] important outside the US? Should the directors of privately owned companies pay the same attention to corporate governance as those that are listed on public exchanges?

In the twenty-first century, corporate governance has become critical for all medium-sized and large organisations. Those without a governance strategy face significant risks; those with one perform measurably better:

Corporations work within a governance framework which is set first by the law and then by regulations emanating from the regulatory bodies to which they are subject. In addition, publicly quoted companies are subject to their shareholders in general meeting and all companies to the forces of public opinion.[5]

Background

The 'greed is good' business philosophy of the 1980s and 1990s seemed to give way, at the end of the twentieth

---

[4] The US Sarbanes-Oxley Act of 2002.
[5] Sir Adrian Cadbury, 'The future for Governance: the Rules of the Game' in *Journal of General Management*, Vol. 24, No.1, Autumn 1998, pp. 1–14.

century, to a 'looting is good' approach. Catastrophic financial failure is, of course, a characteristic of the business cycle and it is not uncommon for a downturn in the cycle to expose organisations that have been playing fast and loose with their shareholders' funds. Warren Buffet has long talked about how a receding economic tide exposes those who have been swimming without any clothes on. Looting has happened before: BICC and Maxwell Communications in the UK are good examples. Corporate collapse, originating in a failure of internal control, has happened before: Baring, again in the UK, is one instance.

The spate of collapses and financial failures at the end of the Internet bubble, though, suggested a systemic weakness, and one whose increasingly worldwide implications had a significant, negative knock-on effect on already problematic pension funds and pensioner assets. Enron, Worldcom, Marconi, Parmalat and many other corporate disasters could be described as the storm damage of unbridled executive authority.

Governments, already grappling with the challenge of funding the pensions of an inexorably greying population bulge, and unwilling to afford further wanton asset destruction, started applying themselves to rooting out corporate misbehaviour. They did this through a combination of overt regulatory action, and slightly more covert pressure on institutional investors to stand up for their rights as shareholders and exercise more determinedly their *de facto* responsibility to insist on proper governance from those organisations in which they were invested.

The concept of governance is a simple one: it 'is the system by which business corporations are directed and controlled'[6]. The 'holy trinity' of good corporate governance has long been seen as shareholder rights, transparency and board accountability.

The global economy recovered rapidly from the slump that followed the bursting of the Internet bubble. It turns out, though, that this recovery was fuelled to an unsustainable extent by a toxic combination of leverage and incomprehensible financial instruments. The financial crash of 2008 and its subsequent recession arose from significant governance, regulatory and risk-management failures in the financial sector, globally. Well-governed corporations are surviving the economic fall-out and their governance of IT plays a significant role in how effectively they compete to survive.

Governance

While corporate governance appears overtly concerned with board structure, executive compensation and shareholder reporting, the underlying assumption is that the board of the corporation is responsible for how the business is managed and for controlling the risks to the organisation's assets and trading future. Across the OECD[7], institutions, investors, regulatory bodies and governments have converged around a common understanding of corporate governance[8] and, in the developing world, corporate governance is increasingly seen as a basic 'cost of entry' into the global capital

---

[6] *OECD Principles of Corporate Governance*, 1999.
[7] The Organisation for Economic Co-operation and Development, an international agency which endeavours to do exactly what its title suggests.
[8] See *IT Governance: Guidelines for Directors*, Alan Calder (IT Governance Publishing, 2005).

markets. The economic turmoil that began in 2008 has increased the importance of governance; well-governed organisations are able to survive and, in the battle of limited investor funds, have a significant competitive advantage.

The term 'Corporate Governance' first gained prominence when it was used by Robert Tricker[9]. He described corporate governance as being 'concerned with the way corporate entities are governed, as distinct from the way businesses within those companies are managed. Corporate governance addresses the issues faced by boards of directors, such as the interaction with top management, and relationships with the owners and others interested in the affairs of the company'[10].

This differentiation – between the governance of a business and its management – is essential to understanding the role of governance in relation to Information and Communications Technology.

The UK, in the Cadbury, Greenbury and Turnbull Reports of the late 1990s, led the way for the OECD in defining how what is known as the directors' duty of care should be exercised. The introduction to the Cadbury report provides a lucid description of the role of corporate governance:

Corporate Governance is the system by which companies are directed and controlled. Boards of directors are responsible for the governance of their companies. The shareholders' role in governance is to appoint the directors and the auditors and to satisfy themselves that an appropriate governance structure is in place. The responsibilities of the board include setting the company's strategic aims, providing the leadership to put them

---

[9] According to Professor Andrew Chambers, in *Tottel's Corporate Governance Handbook* (Tottel Publishing, 2003).

[10] Robert Tricker, *Corporate Governance* (Gower Press, 1984).

into effect, supervising the management of the business and reporting to shareholders on their stewardship. The board's actions are subject to laws, regulations and the shareholders in general meeting.

There are, nevertheless, substantial practical differences between corporate governance frameworks in different jurisdictions. The US corporate governance framework has a far higher degree of compulsion about it than does the UK's 'comply or explain' regime and most continental European and South Asian regimes are, comparatively, still in their infancy. Arguably, the US approach to corporate governance has proved, yet again, to be ineffective as a framework for ensuring that enterprises effectively identify and manage risk. Over-mighty CEOs are a key part of the US problem.

Effective corporate governance is transparent, protects the rights of shareholders, includes both strategic and operational risk management, is as interested in the long-term corporate earning potential as it is in actual short-term earnings and cash flow, holds directors accountable for their stewardship of the business, and ensures that directors exercise their fiduciary duties responsibly. For governance to be effective, boards must consist of a majority of independent directors and be chaired by someone who is strong enough to fire the CEO.

Fiduciary duties

Corporate governance could also be thought of as the combined statutory and non-statutory framework within which boards of directors exercise their fiduciary duties to the organisations that appoint them. The key issue is that 'directors owe to shareholders, or perhaps to the corporation, two basic fiduciary duties: the duty of loyalty and the duty of care'[11].

The duty of care is very important, and the foundation perhaps for the others: it is the duty to pay attention and to try to make good decisions. The decisions do not actually have to be good ones; the directors are simply required to *try* to make good decisions. The United States, for instance, has the 'business judgement rule', also known as the 'doctrine of non-interference'. This allows directors to take business risks, even extreme ones, without fear of legal penalty for failure.

In the United Kingdom, the fiduciary duties of directors were given statutory strength; the Companies Act 2006 identifies seven specific directors' 'general' duties[12]:

1 Duty to act within powers.
2 Duty to promote the success of the company.
3 Duty to exercise reasonable judgement.
4 Duty to exercise reasonable care, skill and diligence.
5 Duty to avoid conflicts of interest.
6 Duty not to accept benefits from third parties.
7 Duty to declare interest in proposed transactions or arrangements.

An eighth duty might be added to these, although it ought to be taken as read: to obey the law and ensure that the company does so, too. Ongoing misdemeanours by companies, both listed and unlisted, suggest that this basic requirement may not be that well understood!

---

[11] Professor Bernard S. Black, Stanford Law School, Presentation at Third Asian Roundtable on Corporate Governance, April 2001.
[12] Companies Act 2006, Chapter 2, paragraphs 170–177.

Governance frameworks

The cost of corporate failure is, in any case, borne by shareholders, by employees, by suppliers, and by other stakeholders in the organisation. There are many current examples of exactly this, ranging from Lehman Brothers to AIG, Woolworths and a slew of construction companies. The groundbreaking Cadbury, Greenbury and Turnbull Reports started by defining how the directors' duty of care – in respect of executive compensation and board management – should be exercised.

Progress has continued. The UK's revised Combined Code is now explicit in saying that all directors are required to 'provide entrepreneurial leadership of the company within a framework of prudent and effective controls which enable risk to be assessed and managed'[13]. This recognises the need for a risk management framework and leaves little room for imprudent risk taking. Directors' duties in the UK have also now been enshrined in statute, as I mentioned earlier.

The US Sarbanes-Oxley Act of 2002 (SOX) required a radical improvement in US corporate governance practices and has cast a long shadow across the world, touching any organisation that has business dealings with US-listed companies. SOX mandated the adoption by US-listed companies of an appropriate system of internal control and, in parallel, required directors to start monitoring and reporting operational risk. SOX, and the associated audit regime, have attracted real interest from within the EU, whose evolving law is significantly influenced by the

---

[13] 'Higgs Suggestions for Good Practice' in *The Combined Code on Corporate Governance* (FSA, January 2003).

experience of SOX. It should be noted that, while SOX has significant internal control implications, it does not have anything like the same focus on effective board governance as does the UK's Combined Code.

Similar governance requirements have emerged elsewhere in the OECD, and the OECD Principles of Corporate Governance, first published in 1999, were revised in 2004.

The spread of the International Financial Reporting Standards (IFRS) across the EU has contributed to a significant convergence in financial reporting and internal control requirements. The ongoing convergence of IFRS and US Generally Accepted Accounting Principles (GAAP) will drive further convergence between auditing, risk management, and corporate governance expectations and practices.

Australia, South Africa and other countries outside the EU already have strong governance frameworks and are taking steps to further strengthen and improve them. Across South Asia and in a number of African and South American countries, the need for effective corporate governance regimes is also being increasingly recognised.

As the tendrils of the corporate governance movement spread out across the financial sphere, and dig deeper into national and international corporate culture, so the pressure on directors to know and understand what is expected of them, and to position themselves for appropriate action – particularly in financially challenging times – is growing.

Emergence of IT governance

The corporate governance of information and communications technology (or IT governance) has, within the broader corporate governance context outlined earlier, become critical for all organisations of any scale. Those that depend on information or intellectual capital, and invest in IT, but do not have an IT governance strategy, are unlikely to be standing in ten years' time.

While corporate governance is overtly concerned with board structure, executive compensation and shareholder reporting, the underlying assumption is, as I have said, that it is the board that is responsible for ensuring that the business strategy is appropriate and that management is effective, and for controlling the risks to the organisation's assets and its trading future.

In today's corporate governance environment, where the value and importance of intellectual assets[14] have become significant, boards must be seen to extend the core governance principles – setting strategic aims, providing strategic leadership, overseeing and monitoring the performance of executive management, and reporting to shareholders on their stewardship of the organisation – to the organisation's intellectual capital, information, and the information and communications technology[15] infrastructure that enables this information to be stored, accessed, shared and manipulated.

A culture of opaqueness is out of line with today's expectation of proactivity and governance transparency. IT

---

[14] These include – but are not limited to – intellectual property such as patents, trademarks, confidential information and know-how. Intellectual assets are referred to, in a balance sheet sense, as Intellectual Capital.
[15] In this guide, we use the term 'IT' inclusively; widespread migration to the internet, 'de-perimeterisation' and the development of the mobile workforce have, between them, advanced the convergence of information and communication technologies to the point where there is little point in trying to think of them as separate, discrete technologies.

is no longer merely a functional or operational issue of concern only to the finance or accounts department. Directors need to be proactive in understanding the strategic importance of, and the operational risks in, their intellectual capital and information technology.

As younger companies, controlled and managed by people who have grown up with IT and its possibilities, transform the business landscape, so those boards that fail to respond to these rapidly changing competitive and environmental pressures can expect their organisations to be destroyed – and whether the destruction is piece by piece, wholesale, immediate or protracted over time is, in the long run, irrelevant.

CHAPTER 1: IT GOVERNANCE DEFINED

Governance, as explained in the Introduction, is distinct from management. Any governance framework – including an IT governance framework — must identify the role of an organisation's governing body, and align that with the governing body's role as described in the OECD Principles of Corporate Governance, revised in 2004, and as originally described in the Cadbury Report on Corporate Governance of 1992.

The UK's revised Combined Code (2004) now explicitly states that all directors are required to 'provide entrepreneurial leadership of the company within a framework of prudent and effective controls which enable risk to be assessed and managed'[16]. This statement recognises the need for a risk management framework and leaves little room for imprudent risk-taking by boards. Directors' duties in the UK have now been enshrined in statute by their explicit inclusion in the Companies Act 2006.

IT governance is a 'framework for the leadership, organisational structures and business processes, standards and compliance to these standards, which ensure that the organisation's IT supports and enables the achievement of its strategies and objectives'[17].

---

[16] 'Higgs Suggestions for Good Practice' in *UK Revised Combined Code* (FSA, January 2003).
[17] Alan Calder, *IT Governance: Guidelines for Directors* (ITGP, 2005). See *www.itgovernance.co.uk/products/19*.

In the future, IT governance will be even more important than corporate governance is today: information and IT are absolutely fundamental to business survival, and organisations that fail to 'direct and control' their IT to best competitive advantage should expect to be left as road kill on the information superhighway.

The five major drivers of IT governance (which are explored further in subsequent chapters) are:

1 The search for competitive advantage in the dynamically changing information economy, through intellectual assets, information and IT.
2 Rapidly evolving governance requirements across the OECD, underpinned by capital market and regulatory convergence.
3 Increasing information- and privacy-related legislation (IT regulatory compliance).
4 The proliferation of threats to intellectual assets, information and IT (and the consequent need for a structured approach to information security and business continuity).
5 The need to align technology projects with strategic organisational goals, ensuring that they deliver planned value (project governance).

ISO/IEC 38500, published in 2008, is the first international standard explicitly addressed to the governing body of an organisation. It deals specifically with the governance of ICT. It recognises that, in smaller organisations, the members of the governing body may also have roles in management. In this way, the standard makes itself applicable to organisations of all sizes, regardless of purpose, design or ownership structure.

Any effective IT governance framework is likely to encompass and include a number of management systems, standards and methodologies, starting with ISO/IEC 38500. Control Objectives for Information Technology (COBIT®), the IT Infrastructure Library® (ITIL®), ISO/IEC 27001 (2005), the Zachman Framework, the Open Group Architecture Framework (TOGAF), PRINCE2™, and M_o_R® are just some of the frameworks and standards that may help an organisation structure its approach to IT governance. The Calder-Moir Framework[18], described in Chapter 12 of this guide onwards, can be described as a meta-model, providing a conceptual approach to organising and deploying this multiplicity of tools; none of these frameworks and standards should overshadow the core responsibility of the board of directors to take forward the governance of IT.

Clearly, for IT governance to be effective within any organisation, board members need to familiarise themselves with their obligations in respect of their organisation's IT; they also need to ensure that they are sufficiently well-informed, *as a body*, to hold their management to account for evolving and delivering an aligned IT strategy that adds significant competitive value to the organisation.

---

[18] See also *www.itgovernance.co.uk/calder_moir.aspx*; a description of this framework together with guidance on its use for organising IT governance can be freely downloaded from this site.

CHAPTER 2: INTELLECTUAL CAPITAL AND THE INFORMATION ECONOMY

The drivers for IT governance have to be understood in the context of the twenty-first century's information, or knowledge, economy, because this economy is fundamentally different from the old manufacturing one. The globalisation of markets, products and resourcing has led to increasingly similar shopping streets selling very much the same products throughout the developed world – and to much of the world experiencing the same economic downturn.

Over 70% of workers in developed economies are now knowledge, rather than manual, workers – including those factory and farm workers whose work depends on understanding and using information technology. Information, networking and telecommunications connectivity make this 'global village' possible – but bring numerous threats and challenges at the same time.

The key characteristics of this global information economy are:

- Information and knowledge are not depleting resources to be protected; on the contrary, sharing knowledge drives innovation.
- Effects of location and time are diminished – virtual organisations now operate round the clock in virtual marketplaces, so that organisations based in east coast America can manufacture in China, handle customer support from India, and sell globally through a single website.

- Laws and taxes are difficult to apply effectively on a national basis as knowledge quickly shifts to low-tax, low-regulation environments.
- Knowledge-enhanced products command price premiums.
- Captured knowledge has a greater intrinsic value than 'knowledge on the hoof'.
- The speed of economic, technological and business change can be extremely fast, has a global footprint and can undermine successful business models virtually overnight.
- Interconnected supply changes bring significant commercial advantages – and significant business risks.

Customer communication and information sharing – particularly through what is known as Web 2.0 sites – can have significant impacts, both positive and negative, on the success or otherwise of global, national and regional brands and businesses.

In a very real sense, knowledge grows as it is shared; more knowledge leads to more innovation, which drives more competition, which in turn drives more globalisation. Greater interconnectedness and the 'always on' economy bring much greater risks.

In the pre-digital manufacturing economy, an organisation's key asset was its productive capability: its machinery, logistical support and distribution equipment, and its stocks of raw materials and finished goods. In the information age, an organisation's key asset is its intellectual capital[19], the combination of its human, structural and market capitals.

Every organisation with a long-term desire to survive and succeed in its chosen market has to focus on preserving, protecting, developing and applying its intellectual capital for the benefit of its shareholders.

Intellectual capital is made up of human, structural and market capital. Simplistically:

- Human capital is made up of the individual competences of the employees in a firm, of its team capabilities, and of knowledge, which includes skills, expertise, experience, and contacts. This knowledge can be both implicit (or tacit: people's know-how) and explicit (that is, it can be documented, in which case it becomes a datum, a piece of information, for someone else).

- Structural capital is made up of the organisation's 'hard' intangible assets (patents, copyrights and other intellectual property, software, databases, documents, methodologies), its standards, attitudes and values, its objectives (particularly strategic), and its processes.

- Market capital is made up of corporate and product branding (including reputation and public perception); supply-chain, partner, and (especially) customer relationships; and market momentum.

There is a high level of interdependence between these three components and they all fundamentally depend on information, knowledge and information technology.

---

[19] The best book on this subject is Thomas A. Stewart's *The Wealth of Knowledge: Intellectual Capital and the 21st Century Organization* (Nicholas Brealey Publishing, 2003), available at *www.itgovernance.co.uk/products/421*.

2: Intellectual Capital and the Information Economy

The Balanced Scorecard system emerged in the late 1990s to provide an 'integrated set of measurements that link current customer, internal process, employee, and system performance to long-term financial success'[20]. It 'translates mission and strategy into objectives and measures, organised into four different perspectives: financial, customer, internal business process, and learning and growth'[21]. There is clearly a correlation between the three non-financial perspectives and the components of intellectual capital, and the Balanced Scorecard has a role to play in the governance and management of IT.

Intellectual capital can be valued. In listed companies, it can be defined, simplistically, as 'an intangible asset that is usually not included on an organisation's balance sheet and which is approximately[22] equal in value to the difference between the market capitalisation of a company and its tangible (or net asset or book) value'[23]. This definition is a pragmatic one; while there are many suggestions, proposals and models, there is no generally accepted and consistently auditable method of accounting for intellectual capital.

Intellectual capital depends, for its productive existence, on information and communication technology: proper IT governance is, therefore, fundamental to both the proper governance and the long-term survival of any twenty-first century organisation.

---

[20] Robert S. Kaplan and David P. Norton, *The Balanced Scorecard: Translating Strategy Into Action* (Harvard Business Press, 1996).
[21] Ibid.
[22] 'Approximately' is an important part of this definition. There are sometimes circumstances in which the market may under- or over-value a company; this is not unusual.
[23] Alan Calder, *IT Governance: Guidelines for Directors* (ITGP, 2005).

CHAPTER 3: STRATEGY: THE SEARCH FOR COMPETITIVE ADVANTAGE

IT is neither low-cost nor low-impact. It is investment-intensive. Innovation in the IT sector is common; speed of innovation and deployment can be critical in developing and maintaining competitive advantage. An organisation must respond proactively to change within its market or see its competitive position eroded and ultimately destroyed. Schumpeter called this process 'Creative Destruction':

[The] process of Creative Destruction is the essential fact about capitalism... every business strategy acquires its true significance only against the background of that process and with the situation created by it. It must be seen in its role in the perennial gale of creative destruction; it cannot be understood irrespective of it or, in fact, on the hypothesis that there is a perennial lull...[24]

IT on its own and of itself is not, however, necessarily a source of competitive advantage. It may be used as such, but in many situations, IT is already commoditised and organisations have to ensure that their systems and processes are as good as (or no worse than) those of their competitors, in order to ensure they do not fall behind in key performance areas.

---

[24] Joseph A. Schumpeter, *Capitalism, Socialism and Democracy* (Harper, 1975), pp. 82–85; organisations are seeing a resurgence in this 'creative destruction' as the global economy tries to recover from the pre-2008 asset-inflation bubble.

IT makes revolutionary business models[25] possible and dramatically transforms the business environment. The challenge of online security slows but does not halt the development of online banking, financial and other e-commerce applications.

The Internet enables small businesses everywhere to compete with larger ones, on a global basis. Digital communication speeds up many aspects of business, including outsourcing, customer awareness and reputation destruction. Green IT, Web 2.0, Software as a Service (SaaS), Cloud Computing, Instant messaging, Voice over IP (VoIP), spyware and sequential auto-responders are technologies as transforming (and disruptive) as Customer Relationship Management (CRM), Human Resource Management (HRM) and Enterprise Resource Planning (ERP) systems were in their day. Of course, the Internet (or Web 2.0) does not replace the need for a real business strategy, or for generating a proper economic return for shareholders; it just transforms the environment within which the board has to create and execute strategy.

It is critical to the survival and ultimate success of their organisations that boards of directors and senior managements put themselves into a position from which they can assess the potential impact on their businesses of emerging and potentially disruptive technologies; they must also themselves be able to understand and oversee in an

---

[25] The term 'business model' '... seems to refer to a loose conception of how a company does business and generates revenue. Yet simply having a business model is an exceedingly low bar to set for building a company. Generating revenue is a far cry from creating economic value, and no business model can be evaluated independently of industry structure. The business model approach to management becomes an invitation for faulty thinking and self-delusion'. Michael E. Porter, 'Strategy and the Internet' in *Harvard Business Review*, March 2001.

effective manner the technology initiatives underway in their own organisations. More than this, boards must be able to ensure that the technology initiatives within their own organisations are driven by the requirements of business strategy, not the other way round.

Development of IT strategy

The board has a key role to play in the development of IT strategy and, by extension, this role plays out in the board's involvement in project governance.

As *Figure 1* over shows, business strategy should drive information strategy; the information required by the organisation should determine the information systems – that is, the applications that will collect, manipulate, store and deliver the information – and these applications should be selected so that application and business process are aligned. The needs of the IS strategy should determine the technology strategy; the technology that is deployed should be what is most suitable for the application and information requirements of the organisation. Of course, there are critical feedback loops: in determining the business strategy, the board needs to be aware of what sort of information can be collected, what sort of applications might be available, and the infrastructure implications of these applications.

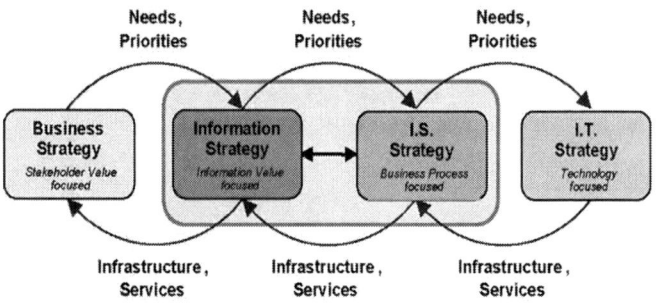

© T.C. Lea-Cox, 1998. Adapted from the work by M.J. Earl, 1989

Figure 1: Development of IT strategy

Business, information and IT strategies

Successful enterprises set their business objectives in the light of the competitive strategy that they have evolved to take advantage of opportunities – or to defend a position – within their specific industry. While the business strategy ought to take into account the organisation's own competences, strengths and weaknesses (relative to those of its competitors), as well as the assets (including intellectual and physical assets) that it can deploy to achieve those goals, it will also generate a requirement for the acquisition or manipulation of specific information – starting with product, market, customer and competitor information – and processes for using that information effectively.

It will also identify the need for specific organisational or business changes to improve the organisation's position regarding its competitors, both those of today and those of tomorrow. The business strategy has measurable goals and investment will be planned to enable the delivery of those goals.

Information strategy

The development of the organisation's information strategy is driven by the business strategy. It is likely that the core of the information strategy will be developed in tandem with the business strategy, because the interrelationship is so close. Creation and completion of a useful intellectual asset register should be a fundamental part of developing a business strategy that seeks to exploit those assets. Of course, once you have such a register, you know what you have to protect and, if you have assigned values to your assets, you know the maximum (less than the replacement value of the asset) you should allow to be spent on that protection.

There is more to an information strategy than simply identifying which information assets to exploit and how to exploit them. Equally important is the identification of the information that will be required to support the organisation in its progress toward its strategic goals. This information ranges from customer and market data through product, financial, human resource, logistic, production and other data, all of which has to be acquired, secured, made available, manipulated and stored. The usual way of determining how information should be managed is to design business processes. Initially high-level, these then have to be translated into detailed, usable tools and procedures.

In most organisations, processes are functionally confined. In other words, there are sales processes, marketing processes, finance processes, HR processes and many others. These processes are traditionally supported by standalone systems, such as customer relationship management (CRM), that work well within the single, vertical information silo, but which do not necessarily work well across the organisation as a whole. One objective of an information strategy might be to break down that vertical separation in order to create integrated cross-functional processes that will speed up data handling while reducing the total processing cost.

The information strategy should, therefore, set out the organisation's objectives for its use of information (for example, a real-time, organisation-wide view of customer data, and end-of-day product- and store-level performance information, or automated just-in-time inventory) to support its business strategy, and should contain a high-level view of the business processes that should deliver those objectives.

IS strategy

The IS strategy is derived from the organisation's information strategy, contains the application strategy, and enables the architecture and infrastructure strategies to be developed. The order of derivation is critical, particularly in existing business environments: it is important to be clear about where you need to go, rather than simply accepting that you are where you are.

The IS strategy will contain high-level views of the processes that the organisation intends to deploy; it is important that these views are platform-independent, and developed without influence from existing application concepts. In other words, neither CRM nor ERP (nor any other application) should be considered as a possible solution until the actual business information and process needs have been objectively defined.

For instance, a business strategy based on differentiation through a very high level of customer care might generate an information strategy requirement for business processes that are designed from the customer back into the organisation, with the objective that it should be possible for anyone in the organisation (from sales through accounts to despatch and logistics) to view information about any customer's transaction through a single user interface (such as a browser) in real time. Out of such an information strategy requirement fall the parameters for the application strategy.

Application strategy

The application strategy's objective is to deliver the requirements of the information strategy and their business processes. The application strategy could reflect an IT implementation principle such as 'use out of the box software; amend processes rather than the software'. While there are many applications available on the market, the organisation needs to set its selection criteria before it examines any of the options. Amongst the criteria should be:

- Alignment with the information strategy requirements – identify which applications come closest, out of the box, to delivering the organisation's information requirements.

- Total cost of ownership (TCO) – the total annual direct (budgeted) and indirect (unbudgeted) cost of acquiring, deploying and owning the software, including the costs of maintenance, upgrades, user training, administration, etc. Products with low initial purchase prices might have significantly higher TCOs.
- Security and compliance – the application must meet the organisation's security and compliance criteria.
- Scalability – the application should have the capacity to support fluctuating numbers of users and evolving user requirements if the organisation's agility is not to be restricted.
- Future-proofing – the application needs to have a reasonable prospect of still being in working shape, and usable by the organisation, at a definable point in the future. This definable point determines the end-point for calculating the Return on Investment (ROI) for the application.

Actual failures of application strategy show up in benchmarking results[26]:

- Organisations use less than 50% of the application software for which they are paying licence fees.
- More than half the software actually used within a standard application is custom software, written by insiders or consultants.
- Interfaces between vendor code and insider custom code show major internal control exposures.
- Maintenance costs of the custom code are usually out of proportion to its value to the organisation.

---

[26] See, for example, West Trax Applications, 'ERP benchmarking results, 2003–2005', reported in *Insight* (the CIMA newsletter), April 2005.

- The CEO and CFO didn't know they had a problem.

IT strategy

In many organisations, the relationship between IT and the business is totally dislocated; it is even more often the case that the IT infrastructure does not support the concept of an 'agile' organisation. Proliferation of technologies and information silos, increasing complexity, and rising costs are common characteristics of many IT infrastructures. Techno-babble and business-unit cynicism about the effectiveness of IT go hand in hand.

Enterprise IT architecture is a simple concept that can bring light into this darkness. It is fundamental to the IT strategy and is a cornerstone of an IT governance framework, but not a substitute for such a framework. Enterprise IT architecture can be defined as a set of organising principles that determine the way in which the organisation's information and communications technology will interact with its operating systems, applications and data. Enterprise architecture is sufficiently important for it to be subject to an enterprise architecture committee; the role of this committee is further discussed in *Chapter 16: Enterprise IT Architecture Committee*.

A number of different architectures exist; the organisation's approach should take the following into account:

- Performance – the organisation's systems need to be robust and able to maintain service levels irrespective of demand (although there may be trade-offs between the costs and benefits of serving extreme demand peaks). The system should be capable of live optimisation to meet changing user numbers and transaction volumes, without bottlenecks.

- Adaptability – as the organisation evolves within its competitive environment, it may need to adapt and modify its processes – its systems should be capable of inexpensive reconfiguration to meet those needs.
- Security and compliance – the security and compliance criteria set by the organisation must be met and, as there are regulatory implications, there must be clear and transparent evidence of this.
- IP ownership models and standards – deployment of proprietary software creates vendor dependence; this may or may not be acceptable. Use of specific standards (of, for instance, data models) should make interoperability of systems less expensive, in both the short term and the long term.
- Information availability – in many organisations, information is stored in vertical silos, and management can get different answers to the same questions from different systems; it would usually be better if there were a consistent presentation of information across all processes and systems.

Application- and hardware-independent service-oriented architectures (SOAs) have evolved to provide business users with a more flexible (usually browser-based) interface than is usually available with monolithic and legacy applications. The benefits of an SOA should include reduced cost and complexity and greater speed in assembling new responses to specific business needs, and an improved return on IT investment through leveraging existing IT resources.

Decisions about ICT can only properly be made in the light of a specific strategy and business plan. Not every organisation needs to deploy architecture x or application y; not every organisation has to be on the cutting edge of technology; not every organisation needs to automate every single one of its processes, or deploy the latest solution pumped by IT vendors. What every organisation needs to do is *what it needs to do* – no more and no less.

Only once an organisation has decided what it needs to do can the board make an informed decision about which information and communications technologies to deploy in its business, or the time-frame over which they should be deployed. The simple fact of the availability of any particular hardware, software, or communications technology is not a good reason to deploy it; an *ab initio* preference for one infrastructural technology over another (open source *versus* proprietary, for instance) could limit the strategic thinking that is fundamental to making the most appropriate enterprise decisions. Once an infrastructural decision is made, the organisation is committed to it for the foreseeable future; changing the infrastructure is a lot harder than simply upgrading it, for many reasons, including the combination of political and financial capital invested in the existing system, the installed user skill base, and business process dependency. Getting this decision right for the business is essential.

The board does not need to get involved in the technical minutiae of any of these decisions; it does, however, need to establish clear principles, guidelines and criteria that relate IT investment decisions to specific business objectives and which enable executives to come forward with proposals that, when implemented, will deliver the business goals.

Of course, the strategic decision-making process does not take place in a vacuum; the board does need to be informed about the ways in which technology is enabling competitors to transform themselves and about the business possibilities offered by new technologies. It also needs to keep the changing technology environment under review, so that it can make early identification of any upcoming changes that might affect its competitive positioning.

Most organisations do not have the opportunity to think their business models through from the outset; they come to IT governance at a time when the organisation already has an installed IT infrastructure which may – or, more often, may not – be fit for the business purpose. Such an IT infrastructure has 'evolved' because there has been no effective governance of IT.

It is nevertheless important that an appropriate IT strategy development process is developed and established as early as possible, and that it is clearly understood by senior management (and particularly by business and functional managers). Such an approach will enable the organisation to shift, over a period of time, to effective alignment of IT strategy and investment with business strategy and strategic goals.

The six-step IT strategy process

Risk management and implementation also have roles to play. The development and implementation of the four-stage IT strategy described earlier is, therefore, a six-step process:

- Step 1: the board establishes and agrees the business strategy. This stage is outside the scope of this book.

- Step 2: the executive team identifies the information requirements ('What information do we need, where do we get it from, how are we going to process and use it?').
- Step 3: the executive team develops the IS or application requirements ('What business processes do we need?' 'What software will enable us to do this?'). This is also an appropriate time to consider the IT services that might be required to support the information and application strategies. (See *Information strategy* and *IS strategy* earlier in this chapter.)
- Step 4: the IT architecture committee documents the proposed architecture, reflecting the agreed IT principles and the information and application requirements; this enables a technology committee to identify the operating system, hardware and communication technology platforms, and user access devices that will support the application and information requirements. (See *Chapter 16: Enterprise IT Architecture Committee.*)
- Step 5: the technology committee applies the board's risk treatment and compliance/security criteria to the cumulative output of steps 2 to 4 and makes any changes necessary to bring the draft IT strategy into conformance with these criteria. (Risk management frameworks are discussed in *Chapter 4: Governance and Risk Management.*)
- Step 6: the executive team ensures that required competences and resources have been identified, and that financial and risk criteria have all been met, and then approves the proposed IT strategy and puts it to the board for approval.

Measurement and quality

A fundamental aspect of any meaningful IT governance framework is the measurement of IT activity. Measurement of IT is also one of the many areas in which businesses have traditionally failed in their governance responsibilities. Decisions about what to measure should be made alongside the development of the business strategy, and should be embedded in the process of translating strategic business needs into IS strategy and, ultimately, IT strategy.

The Balanced Scorecard, which is now widely used in organisations across the world, can be extended to the IT function. In organisations that already use the Balanced Scorecard, this will not be a revolutionary step. Organisations that do not currently use the Balanced Scorecard can deploy it within the IT function without having first used it elsewhere in the organisation.

The IT Balanced Scorecard

Measurement matters: "If you can't measure it, you can't manage it." An organization's measurement system strongly affects the behaviour of people both inside and outside the organization. If companies are to survive and prosper in information age competition, they must use measurement and management systems derived from their strategies and capabilities. Unfortunately, many organizations espouse strategies about customer relationships, core competencies, and organizational capabilities while motivating and measuring performance only with financial measures. The Balanced Scorecard retains financial measurement as a critical summary of managerial and business performance, but it highlights a more general and integrated set of measurements that link current customer, internal process, employee, and system performance to long-term financial success.[27]

Measurement matters even more in IT; after decades of over-promising and under-delivering, measurement that pertains to the organisation's goals and to the contribution that IT makes to achieving them is essential. The Balanced Scorecard has increasingly been deployed over the last five years for managing IT organisations. In early 2001, Robert Gold[28] identified four key lessons important for IT leaders when developing an IT Balanced Scorecard. These were:

1   Set the agenda: concisely define the IT organisation's objectives and communicate them clearly to stakeholders, seeking to showcase the IT unit's performance, offset criticism, or integrate the Balanced Scorecard with IT team performance management.

2   Involve business-unit managers in defining the IT strategy, preferably in moving from proving business competency to contributing to value creation in the business units.

3   Align IT spending and investment plans with business-unit expectations, ensuring that, where budget factors are outside the IT organisation's control, these are clearly understood and the IT organisation's performance is focused around delivering required value within the budget constraints.

4   Commit to change: the benefits of implementing an IT Balanced Scorecard take a long time to show through and will require behavioural change at all levels in the IT

---

[27] Robert S. Kaplan and David P. Norton, *The Balanced Scorecard: Translating Strategy into Action* (HBS Press, 1996).
[28] Robert S. Gold, *Building the IT Organization Balanced Scorecard* (HBS Publishing, 2002).

organisation. It is important that everyone in the IT team commits to the required changes and will 'stick with it'.

Perspectives

The generic Balanced Scorecard has four perspectives: financial, customer, internal, and learning and growth. An IT organisation might make use of these perspectives in the following way:

1 Financial: budget management, return on investment (taking into account all IT projects, successes and failures), enterprise total cost of ownership (TCO), IT intensity (ratio of headcount to IT investment at original cost), intangible relevance (ratio of intellectual capital value to total organisational capitalisation)[29].

2 Customer (internally): user satisfaction (system efficiency – the measures used in internal and external service level agreements (SLAs) could be consolidated here), cost-effective/competitive sourcing and delivery, speed of solution delivery, innovations that create business value. This perspective could probably also include regulatory and statutory compliance reporting.

3 Internal (to IT organisation) processes: implementation of enterprise IT architecture, reduction of system conflicts, reliability and functionality of systems, data integrity, system and information availability, response times, costs, new product development, management of outsourced IT operations, project governance, etc. This perspective could also include regulatory compliance

---

[29] See Chapter 3 of Alan Calder, *IT Governance: Guidelines for Directors* (ITGP, 2005), available at *www.itgovernance.co.uk/products/19.*

relating, for instance, to data protection and privacy, information security, and business continuity.

4 Learning and growth: IT organisation staff satisfaction, IT skills and competences in relation to those required to achieve the organisation's IT strategy, managerial skills and competences.

The Baldridge National Quality Program's Criteria for Performance Excellence provides a rich source of input for the type of measurements that might be used in the IT organisation Balanced Scorecard. Every organisation will have to develop and apply its own IT Balanced Scorecard. It must be developed specifically to suit the requirements of each organisation and must certainly be integrated with the whole-organisation version of the Balanced Scorecard (if one exists) if the IT version is to be a genuinely useful tool.

Balanced Scorecard implementation

Of course, implementation of an effective measurement process may, initially, be a politically sensitive step. Many in the IT organisation may fear the implication that their performance has been inadequate, and some of the senior IT leaders may resent the loss of day-to-day operational power that is such an inescapable component of any effective board-led measurement framework. Implementation of a measurement framework, a quality management process, is not a new business skill; there already exists substantial guidance on and experience of the introduction and management of change, and such guidance would certainly be worth following when introducing an effective measurement system.

CHAPTER 4: GOVERNANCE AND RISK MANAGEMENT

Risk management has always been a key governance issue. The board's job is strategy and, therefore, strategic risk has always been a board responsibility, and effective risk management has become a key competitive differentiator. The modern corporation's fundamental goal is to create and add value to its business on a continual basis. This means that boards must find an appropriate balance between profit maximisation and risk reduction.

Strategic risk can be described as the enterprise-level risk of a negative impact on earnings or capital arising from an organisation's failure to create and execute appropriate business plans and strategies, improper implementation of decisions, or lack of responsiveness to industry changes. It includes risks associated with plans for entering new businesses, for expanding existing services, for mergers, acquisitions and divestments, and for enhancing the infrastructure.

The two key strategic risks related to information and communications technology are:

1 Interruptions (whether from project failure or unplanned disruption) to business processes and customer services.
2 Overspending on IT, placing the company at a cost disadvantage compared to its competitors.

Both these risks should be dealt with as part of the strategic risk management process.

In the last few years, the parallel importance of operational risk ('the risk of direct or indirect loss resulting from inadequate or failed internal processes, people and systems or from external events'[30]) has, driven by the Basel II process in the global financial sector, also been recognised.

Enterprise risk management[31]

Risk assessment has become a pervasive (and sometimes invasive) concept: a risk assessment must be structured and formal, and nowadays one is expected in almost every context, from a school outing through to a major corporate acquisition. It is certainly a cornerstone of today's corporate governance regimes. In the context of both strategic and operational risk, risk identification and assessment are the first steps that a board should take in controlling the risks facing the organisation. The most important step is the development of a risk treatment plan (in which risks are accepted, controlled, eliminated or contracted out) that is appropriate in the context of the company's strategic objectives.

Controls are the countermeasures for risks and, in a practical sense, the development of an IT governance framework is a control that enables an organisation to mitigate the strategic IT risks in its business model and strategy.

---

[30] 'Operational Risk', a consultative document from the Basel Committee on Banking Supervision, published in January 2001.
[31] It is not the purpose of this manual to discuss ERM frameworks at any length; the best resource for ERM guidance is the COSO *Enterprise Risk Management – Integrated Framework*. See *www.coso.org/Publications/ERM/COSO_ERM_ExecutiveSummary.pdf*.

Operational risk management

The key components of an effective approach to operational risk management will be consistent, and will include:

- A clear, board-driven operational risk strategy with meaningful review, oversight and monitoring.
- A strong internal control and operational risk management culture (which includes clear segregation of duties and clear lines of responsibility).
- Effective internal reporting.
- Meaningful contingency planning.

Sound risk-management practice includes:

- The development of policies, processes and procedures that will implement the board's strategy.
- Effective communication up and down the organisation.
- Identification and quantification of risks in all current activities, processes, systems and in new products.
- Systems for monitoring operational risk exposures.
- Cost/benefit analysed policies, processes and procedures for controlling or mitigating operational risk.
- Independent evaluation and reporting on these various systems, processes and procedures.

The corporate governance framework – and, by extension, the IT governance framework – should have exactly these characteristics.

IT risk management

IT risk management has become a hot IT topic over the last few years. As organisations become increasingly dependent on information technology and intellectual capital assets, the key areas of IT (operational) risk are usually seen as:

- IT infrastructure and network security – arising from concerns about hackers, terrorists, cyber-criminals, insiders, outsiders, viruses, malware, phishing, and so on, all of which might be classified under the heading of 'information risk'.

- Data integrity, confidentiality, privacy and compliance – arising from regulatory and market pressure to protect both personal data (for example, data protection legislation) and corporate data (for example, fair disclosure regulations), as well as financial and operational data (such as Sarbanes-Oxley). This might be called 'compliance risk'.

- Business continuity and disaster recovery – arising from concerns about the organisation's capability to continue in business after a natural or man-made disaster. This might be called 'continuity risk'.

- IT management issues – arising from concerns about project failure, poor IT operational performance, inadequate IT infrastructure, etc. all of which is sometimes called 'management risk'.

The effects of these risks are not limited to the IT department; their impact is felt across the entire organisation and they must therefore be managed within the enterprise risk management framework. IT risks should form their own category on the corporate risk register; the key IT risks should be identified and owned within a coherent IT governance framework that is itself fully integrated into the organisation, and which enables the board to govern IT within the context of the overall business model, strategy and risk management framework.

CHAPTER 5: IT REGULATORY COMPLIANCE

Information is increasingly subject to legislation. Customers, staff, suppliers, tribunals and law courts all expect organisations to comply with this legislation in a proactive manner. Legislation and regulation exist on national, international, and industry-specific levels. Most OECD countries have some form of data protection and privacy legislation. National regulations often overlap and are sometimes contradictory, and almost all of them lack implementation guidance or adequate precision. Copyright, digital rights, computer misuse and electronic trading legislation are changing rapidly, and legislation on money laundering, proceeds of crime, human rights and freedom of information all add to the confusion.

Organisations also have to respond to regulatory and contractual requirements; the Payment Card Industry Data Security Standard (PCI DSS), for instance, is a private standard, applied and enforced through bank-merchant contracts. Its requirements have to be met alongside sector regulations and national laws about the protection of personally identifiable information.

Complex organisations, with diversified or (partially) virtual business models, operating in and across a number of legal jurisdictions, have an even more complex task. While any one regulation (and its related compliance issues) might apply only to a subsidiary national entity, it is the global parent whose reputation might be damaged, and the more failures, the more damage.

While fines and the personal liability of directors and officers can appear as significant risks in relation to some –

but not all – of this legislation, not all of the regulatory bodies have historically had the resources and capability to be proactive about investigating and pursuing possible transgressors.

Things are changing. Earlier this decade, a New York attorney general expressed a common view when he said: 'the honour code amongst CEOs didn't work. Board oversight didn't work. Self-regulation was a complete failure'[32]. The most recent UK legislation (the 2006 Companies Act), the current revision to the European Union's 8th Company Law Directive on Statutory Audit, and the changes to data protection legislation across the world, all point to greater compulsion – from governments, regulators and justice departments – towards compliance requirements becoming the norm across the OECD.

The need for regulatory compliance should not be allowed to disable the organisation, but neither should it be ignored. Shareholders do not expect their companies to be in breach of national or international regulations.

Regulatory compliance and risk management appear to go hand in hand. The best companies have always addressed strategic risk and regulatory compliance from the boardroom. For today's international organisation the Unified Compliance Framework (UCF)[33] provides a structured and coherent compliance matrix that cross-references hundreds of information and IT-related regulations from across the OECD. The UCF also has a key

---

[32] Eliot Spitzer, interviewed in *Wall Street Journal*, 8 April 2005.
[33] See Dorian J. Cougias, Marcelo Halpern, and Rebecca Herold, *Say What You Do: Building a Framework of IT Controls, Policies, Standards, & Procedures* (Network Frontiers, 2007), available at *www.itgovernance.co.uk/products/1436* .

role to play in a properly-structured IT governance framework.

Information security law: the emerging standard for corporate compliance[34]

Within the overall regulatory compliance environment, information security is rapidly emerging as a critical legal issue. As the list of highly publicised security breaches[35] suffered by reputable companies, organisations, and government agencies continues to expand at an exponential rate, it is becoming clear that all corporate data is vulnerable.

The increasing legal and regulatory focus on information security stems from the fact that, in today's business environment, virtually all of a company's daily transactions and all of its key records are created, used, communicated, and stored in electronic form using networked computer technology. Most business entities are dependent upon information technology and an interconnected information infrastructure.

While this has provided companies with tremendous economic benefits, including significantly reduced costs and increased productivity, the resulting dependence on electronic records and a networked computer infrastructure creates significant potential vulnerabilities that can result in

---

[34] See Thomas Smedinghoff, *Information Security Law: The Emerging Standard for Corporate Compliance* (ITGP, 2008), which can be found at *www.itgovernance.co.uk/products/1975*. The text in this section paraphrases the introduction to, and another section of, this book.

[35] See *http://attrition.org/dataloss* for details of reported database breaches that affect personal data.

major harm to the business and to its stakeholders[36]. Creating, communicating and storing corporate information in electronic form greatly enhances the potential for unauthorised access, use, disclosure, and alteration, as well as the risk of accidental loss or destruction.

Concerns regarding corporate governance, individual privacy, accountability for financial information, the authenticity and integrity of transaction data, and the protection of sensitive business data are driving the enactment of laws and regulations designed to ensure that businesses adequately address the security of their own data. These legislative and regulatory initiatives are imposing obligations on all businesses to implement information security measures to protect their own data and, already in the US and potentially elsewhere in the world, to disclose breaches of security that do occur.

In particular, businesses need to understand and address three legal trends that are rapidly shaping the global information security landscape and defining the requirements that businesses must satisfy. They are:

- An expanding duty to provide security for corporate data.
- The emergence of a legal standard for compliance.
- The imposition of a new duty to warn those adversely affected by a security breach.

Although the law is still developing, and is often applied only in selective areas, these trends are posing significant

---

[36] 'As a result of increasing interconnectivity, information systems and networks are now exposed to a growing number and a wider variety of threats and vulnerabilities. This raises new issues for security.' OECD Guidelines for the Security of Information Systems and Networks, 25 July 2002, page 7. See *www.oecd.org/dataoecd/16/22/15582260.pdf*.

new challenges for most businesses, all of which are fully explored in Thomas Smedinghoff's important book[37] on this subject, which argues that ISO/IEC 27001 is emerging as the legal standard for corporate compliance to these legal requirements.

ISO27001 is a relatively new international standard (published in October 2005). Smedinghoff says that it has the appearance of a trustworthy standard, given the process by which it was prepared. Smedinghoff argues that the standard offers important advantages, stating that while ISO27001 is a technical standard for information security, it appears to be based on essentially the same premise as the legal standard for information security contained in existing legislation and outlined in Chapters 4, 5 and 6 of his book. That is, ISO27001 'adopts a process approach to establishing, implementing, operating, monitoring, reviewing, maintaining, and improving an organisation's Information Security Management System (ISMS)'[38].

ISO27001 also includes all of the requirements of the legal standard – it requires companies to identify their information assets[39], to conduct risk assessments[40], to select responsive security controls[41], to implement and operate their information security management system (ISMS)[42], to monitor and review their ISMS[43], to maintain and improve their ISMS[44], and also to manage the security of third

---

[37] Thomas Smedinghoff, *Information Security Law: The Emerging Standard for Corporate Compliance* (ITGP, 2008). See *www.itgovernance.co.uk/products/1975*.
[38] ISO27001, § 0.2.
[39] Ibid. § 4.2.1.
[40] Ibid.
[41] Ibid.
[42] Ibid. § 4.2.2.
[43] Ibid. §§ 4.2.3 and 6.
[44] Ibid. §§ 4.2.4 and 8.

parties[45]. Smedinghoff argues that the adoption of ISO27001 by two international standards groups comprised of representatives from most countries – ISO and IEC – represents at least a tacit endorsement of the legal standard for security at an international level. Moreover, although compliance with the ISO27001 standard does not guarantee legal compliance (it is not a safe harbour)[46], it may offer companies a good starting point on the road to addressing international legal requirements for security.

ISO27001 is an auditable standard. Compliance with the standard can be certified by a third party qualified to do ISO27001 audits. This is because ISO27001 provides a specification for an ISMS, which is, in essence, similar to the concept of a comprehensive information security programme as defined in many current security statutes and regulations. It adopts a process approach[47] that is very similar to the approach for the legal standard for security discussed in Smedinghoff's book.

ISO27001 is an essential component of any organisation's approach to achieving compliance with information-related regulation; it is also an essential component of any IT governance framework.

---

[45] Ibid. § A.10.2.
[46] ISO27001 itself specifically states that 'Compliance with an International Standard does not in itself confer immunity from legal obligations' (page 1).
[47] ISO27001, § 0.2.

CHAPTER 6: INFORMATION AND CONTINUITY RISK

Organisational information is an asset and therefore, by definition, someone outside the organisation will want it; if no-one wanted it, it wouldn't be an asset. If it is to be useful to an organisation, information must:

- be available (to those who need to use it).
- be confidential (so that competitors can't use it).
- have its integrity guaranteed (so that it can be relied upon).

Information risk arises from the threats – both external and internal – to the availability, confidentiality and integrity of the organisation's information assets. Organisations must address direct risks to the availability, confidentiality and integrity of their information; they also need to address continuity risks to their business operations and IT infrastructure.

Information risks and ISO27001

Headline figures have long illustrated the cost of security failures: the UK's National High Tech Crime Unit (NHTCU) reported that 89% of firms interviewed had suffered some form of computer crime in the previous 12 months (up from 83% in the previous year), at a cost of at least £2.4 billion[48].

Threats to information security are wide-ranging, complex and costly. External threats include:

- Casual criminals (virus writers, hackers).
- Organised crime (virus writers, hackers, spammers, phishers, fraudsters, espionage, ex-employees).
- Terrorists (including anarchists).

Securing information against cybercrime, cyberwar and cyberterrorism[49] should be high on corporate agendas.

More information security incidents originate inside the organisation than outside it. Such incidents might involve members of staff, contractors and consultants, acting either maliciously or carelessly. White-collar crime is, nowadays, largely computer-based. Baring, Enron, WorldCom and Arthur Andersen were all brought down by insiders.

The indirect costs of information security incidents such as loss of card holders' details or other customer personal data usually far exceed their direct ones, and the reputational impacts are often even greater.

There is, of course, a crossover between compliance and information risk: when HMRC in the UK mislaid a number of CD-ROMs, it was in breach of its obligations under the Data Protection Act 1998; it may also have fed a fast-

---

[48] *Hi-Tech Crime: the Impact on UK Business 2005*, survey conducted by NOP for the UK's NHTCU. The NHTCU was merged into SOCA (the Serious and Organised Crime Agency) shortly after publishing this report.

[49] For authoritative coverage of this subject, see Dr Julie Mehan, *CyberWar, CyberTerror, CyberCrime* (available at *www.itgovernance.co.uk/products/1731*).

growing criminal underworld which thrives on reselling individually identifiable data.

Boards should use their IT governance frameworks to assure themselves that all of their information-related risks have been identified and appropriately controlled. Accredited certification to the international information security management standard, ISO/IEC 27001:2005 (which we have already discussed in the context of legal compliance), is the most effective way of achieving this. Controlling information risk is a powerful reason for ISO27001 certification to be an integral part of an IT governance framework.

Continuity risks and BS25999, ISO/IEC 24762

Business continuity and disaster recovery planning is another key governance responsibility. The UK Companies Act 2006 gives statutory force to what has long been the worldwide common-law duty of directors, which is to exercise due care in relation to their companies. Specifically, directors must 'exercise reasonable care, skill and diligence'[50].

The board of directors is accountable for ensuring that the organisation has developed and tested business continuity and disaster recovery plans that deal with all the likely risks that face the organisation.

Research suggests that 80% of organisations with a tried and tested business continuity plan are likely to survive a major business discontinuity, while only 20% of those

---

[50] UK Companies Act 2006, §174.

without such a plan are likely to find a way of overcoming a disaster and continuing in business. Business continuity is not just an IT and data issue; it is an issue for the whole organisation. Possible continuity risks include the loss of telecommunications, of internet connectivity, of physical premises, of machinery or equipment, or of critical people. And while business continuity planning is not the same as disaster recovery planning, the two are closely related.

Business resilience is another term ascribed to this area of operational risk control. CERT has developed a Resiliency Engineering Framework (REF)[51], which it describes as 'a capability model for operational resiliency management'[52]. It was designed with two primary objectives:

1 Establish the convergence of operational risk and resiliency management activities such as security, business continuity, and aspects of IT operations management, into a single model.
2 Apply a process improvement approach to operational resiliency management through the definition and application of a capability level scale that expresses increasing levels of process improvement.

In fact, CERT describes REF as a meta-model that includes references to other standards and best practices, including ISO27001, BS25999 and others.

BS25999[53] (which replaced PAS56 on 27 November 2006) is the best practice standard for business continuity plans and every organisation should, for its own survival, follow

---

[51] The framework can be downloaded from
www.cert.org/resiliency_engineering/framework.html.
[52] www.cert.org/resiliency_engineering.
[53] Copy available at www.itgovernance.co.uk/products/1363.

as much of the BS25999 guidance as is appropriate for its specific circumstances. BS25999 supports Chapter 14 of ISO27001, which deals extensively with the information security aspects of business continuity planning.

ISO/IEC 24762 is an international standard developed specifically to provide guidance around IT disaster recovery. It aids the operation of an ISO27001 information security management system (ISMS) with guidance on the provision of information and communications technology disaster recovery (ICT DR) services as part of the overall business continuity management plan.

Civil contingencies and business continuity planning

In the UK, the Civil Contingencies Act 2004[54] sets out specific requirements for public bodies. It imposes a series of duties on local bodies in England and Wales, Scotland, and Northern Ireland (who are known as 'Category 1 responders'). These duties include assessing the risk of an emergency occurring and maintaining plans for the purposes of responding to an emergency. The range of Category 1 responders is broader than the range of local bodies which were subject to earlier legislation (which has now been repealed). It includes:

- Certain bodies with functions which relate to health.
- The Environment Agency.
- The Secretary of State, in so far as his functions relate to responding to maritime and coastal emergencies.

---

[54] See *www.opsi.gov.uk/Acts/acts2004/ukpga_20040036_en_1*.

The Act also provides the mechanism to impose duties on other local bodies ('Category 2 responders') to co-operate with, and provide information to, Category 1 responders in connection with their civil protection duties.

In summary, business resilience – business continuity and disaster recovery – is as important a component of a governance framework as information security.

CHAPTER 7: INTERNAL CONTROL FRAMEWORKS

Internal control frameworks have traditionally been designed to deal primarily with financial risk: the risk that errors or dishonesty could lead to loss of corporate money. From a corporate governance perspective, it is now increasingly understood that internal controls must respond to the much wider range of risks identified within the organisation's enterprise risk management (ERM) framework.

UK-based companies look primarily to the Turnbull Guidance on internal control and, while the work done on internal control frameworks by the international Treadway Commission and the US Public Company Accounting Oversight Board (PCAOB)[55] are more directly relevant to US-listed companies they are also, because of their widespread impacts, key reference points outside the US.

UK Combined Code and Turnbull Guidance

The UK's Combined Code requires listed companies to review annually 'all material controls, including financial, operational and compliance controls, and risk management systems'[56]. The Turnbull Guidance explicitly requires boards, on an ongoing basis, to identify, assess and deal

---

[55] www.pcaobus.org.
[56] Combined Code on Corporate Governance, §C.2.1.

with significant risks in all areas, including in information and communications processes[57].

Sarbanes-Oxley

The Sarbanes-Oxley Act of 2002 (SOX) requires US-listed companies to assess annually the effectiveness of their internal controls, the CEO and CFO to certify annually the adequacy of these internal controls, and the external auditors to attest to this. Section 409 requires companies to disclose to the public 'on a rapid and current basis such additional information concerning material changes in the financial condition or operations of the issuer'.

Financial reporting depends critically on the IT infrastructure, whether it is for the rendering of an invoice, the effective operation of an ERP system, or an integrated, organisation-wide management information and control system. If management is to be in a position where it can show that the organisation's accounts are materially correct, it must assure itself that appropriate internal controls exist, and that they are operating as intended; it is not sufficient (in the UK) to rely on the finance director for a representation made by the directors as a body.

COSO and internal control

The Committee of Sponsoring Organisations (COSO) defines internal control broadly as:

...a process, effected by an entity's board of directors, management and other personnel, designed to provide

---

[57] *Turnbull Guidance*, paragraph 20.

reasonable assurance regarding the achievement of objectives in the following categories:

- Effectiveness and efficiency of operations
- Reliability of financial reporting
- Compliance with applicable laws and regulations.

The first category addresses an entity's basic business objectives, including performance and profitability goals and safeguarding of resources. The second relates to the preparation of reliable published financial statements, including interim and condensed financial statements and selected financial data derived from such statements, such as earnings releases, reported publicly. The third deals with complying with those laws and regulations to which the entity is subject.[58]

The definition is a good one. COSO says, and most accounting organisations would agree, that internal control consists of five inter-related elements. These are:

1 The control environment – the foundation for all other elements, influencing the control consciousness of the people within the organisation, and encompassing every aspect of how the organisation is structured and works, from the attention and direction provided by the board through to the ethical values and competence of the staff.

2 Risk assessment – the identification and analysis of risks to the achievement of the organisation's business objectives.

3 Control activities – these are the policies and procedures that help the organisation's board and management ensure that their control decisions are carried out in relation to identified risks; they occur at all levels and in all parts of the organisation and include, for instance,

---

[58] *Internal Control – Integrated Framework: Executive Summary*, available at www.coso.org.

authorisations, reviews, duty segregation and reconciliations.

4 Information and communication – these must occur at two levels:

- The board must communicate its control objectives clearly to staff throughout the organisation (as well as to external parties), and staff must be able to communicate effectively with management.

- The organisation's information systems must capture and report pertinent information (operational, financial and compliance-related as well as external activities and conditions that affect the business) in a time-frame and format that enable the organisation's board and management to carry out their responsibilities.

5 Monitoring – the ongoing monitoring of internal control systems includes regular and *ad hoc* functional and management reviews, and should be based on a risk assessment, with serious deficiencies reported to management and the board.

COSO identifies two broad groups of IT systems control activities: general controls and application controls. General controls ensure that the financial information from a company's application systems can be relied upon. These controls exist most commonly as part of an information security management system (such as that identified in SO27002) or an IT controls system such as Control Objectives for Information Technology (COBIT). Application controls are embedded in the software to detect or prevent unauthorised transactions. Such controls can be used to ensure the completeness, accuracy, validity and authorisation of transactions.

COBIT

The Information Systems Audit and Control Association (ISACA)[59] has produced COBIT[60], a widely used framework for auditing IT governance. COBIT is increasingly accepted as a good-practice framework for control of information, IT and related risks. Its guidance helps organisations implement effective governance over enterprise-wide IT. In particular, COBIT's management guidelines component contains a framework for the control and measurability of IT by providing tools to assess and measure the enterprise's IT capability for 34 identified IT processes.

ISACA has developed guidance that enables COBIT to be applied to the specific internal control objectives of identified legislation, and which looks at specific software systems. The following guidance is available for download from the ISACA website[61]:

- IT Control Objectives for Basel II.
- IT Control Objectives for Sarbanes-Oxley.
- Managing Risk in a Wireless Environment: Security, Audit and Control Features.
- Security, Audit and Control Features Oracle E-Business Suite (Second Edition).
- Security, Audit and Control Features PeopleSoft (Second Edition).
- Security, Audit and Control Features SAP R/3 (Second Edition).

---

[59] www.isaca.org.
[60] COBIT 4.1, developed by ISACA. Copies of COBIT are available from ISACA (www.isaca.org) or from www.itgovernance.co.uk/catalog/40.
[61] www.isaca.org/bookstore.

COBIT's strength is at the overall IT process level; it does not provide the level of precision that more specialised standards – such as ISO/IEC 27001:2005 for information security management, ISO/IEC 20000:2006 for IT Service Management and BS25999 for business continuity management – do in each of their specific areas or around specific control areas.

Clearly, any IT governance framework must include the appropriate internal control elements to enable boards to assure themselves, and regulators, that they are meeting their compliance obligations.

Val IT

Val IT is another IT governance framework developed by ISACA. Val IT addresses the governance of IT-enabled business investments and consists of a set of guiding principles and a number of processes conforming to those principles that are further defined as a set of key management practices.

The Val IT framework, which is written to be compatible with COBIT 4.1, is supported by publications[62] and operational tools and provides guidance on how to:

- define the relationship between IT, the business and those functions in the organisation with governance responsibilities.
- manage an organisation's portfolio of IT-enabled business investments.

---

[62]See *www.itgovernance.co.uk/products/895.*

- maximise the quality of business cases for IT-enabled business investments with particular emphasis on the definition of key financial indicators, the quantification of 'soft' benefits and the comprehensive appraisal of the downside risk.

Val IT addresses assumptions, costs, risks and outcomes that relate to a balanced portfolio of IT-enabled business investments. It also provides benchmarking capability and allows enterprises to exchange experiences on best practices for value management.

CHAPTER 8: PROJECT GOVERNANCE

The fast-changing information economy drives organisations to continuous information innovation. This, combined with relentless cost pressure, drives them on to attempt continuous system and process improvement. Increasingly, organisations 'bet the farm' on the successful development and deployment of new systems, in a business environment that can change so fast that the original assumptions on which a project's rationale were based can become fatally undermined before the project has been completed.

These projects have ceased to be IT projects; they are complex 'whole business' projects, with varied impacts across the business as a whole, requiring input and resource from many areas other than the IT department. They are too important to the strategic health of the organisation to be left to the IT department or to be the management responsibility of one person alone.

In both the public and private sectors, IT-enabled business projects are critical to the organisation's business model and strategy. Stakeholders believe that IT-related projects should deliver measurable business benefits, and boards need a framework that will enable informed reporting to stakeholders.

Organisations should use a capability maturity model[63] to assess their current level of project management maturity

---

[63] See Chapter 6 of Alan Calder, *IT Governance Today: a Practitioner's Handbook* (IT Governance Publishing, 2005).

and to provide a road map for how they want to develop what should be a core organisational competence over time.

Project failure

There are multiple reasons for project failure. There is only one for project success: good governance. The 1995 Chaos Report identified how much money was wasted in one year alone:

- Only 16% of software projects were completed on time and on budget.
- 31% of projects were cancelled before completion.
- 53% of projects would cost over 189% of their original estimates.

More recent surveys indicate that nothing much has changed. Even in those organisations that take a reasonably structured, traditional approach to project governance, the sheer complexity and scale of IT-related business projects means that such projects are still likely to fail.

While newspaper headlines identify project failure in the public sector, private-sector failures are usually brushed under the carpet until the organisation's underperformance forces the board to accept change – usually of the CEO and other senior management.

Project governance objectives

No large-scale or business-critical project should ever be managed on a standalone basis. If there is to be organisation-wide buy-in, a governance approach is essential. Project governance has six interlinked objectives:

1 Ensuring real business value through project and business alignment.
2 Controlling cost through centralisation.
3 Maximising resource utilisation (particularly high value resources).
4 Risk management through portfolio balancing.
5 Uniform application of best practice.
6 Organisational coherence.

Of course, the organisation needs to have chosen an overall approach to project management that is appropriate to its project objectives and development environment. 'Agile' methodologies, for instance, can be more effective for software development than traditional 'big bang' approaches[64].

Execution risk

The board must plan for execution risk[65] at four levels: strategic (or corporate), programme, project and operational. Each level of risk needs appropriate risk treatment plans, and these should be identified in the context of an overall corporate risk treatment plan.

Executive-level project governance

The organisation's executive is responsible for the execution of any project, within clearly understood parameters. The executive needs to customise the organisational structure to ensure project success and,

---

[64] See Alan Calder, *IT Governance Today: a Practitioner's Handbook* (IT Governance Publishing, 2005), Chapter 6.
[65] Ibid.

above all, must make sure that board and senior management support of the project is clearly understood and communicated throughout the organisation. A critical path analysis, adequate resourcing, and an appropriate project management methodology are prerequisites.

Board-level project governance

IT investment decisions (for *or* against) expose an organisation to significant risks, which can be financial, operational and/or competitive. The board must insist that project risks are assessed within the organisation's strategic planning and risk management framework and ensure that the right investment and management decisions, the ones which enhance competitive advantage and deliver measurable business value, are made. Critically, projects need continual oversight; the assumptions on which they were predicated need continual reassessment and the expected benefits need regular reappraisal. Ultimate accountability for the effective management of the project portfolio must rest with the board as a whole, rather than with any one individual.

The board therefore has a specific project governance role, comprising the following:

- The board approves project initiation, manages the project portfolio and pulls the plug on under- or non-performing projects.
- One or more non-executive board members must be specifically responsible for overseeing project governance. They must have independent, informed oversight of progress on all business IT projects – and must attend programme (or large project) board meetings.

8: Project Governance

- Accountability must be clearly identified at all levels, with detailed, rigorously tested project plans based on a critical path analysis with clearly identified critical success factors, regular milestones, and 'go-no-go' checkpoints.
- The board must ensure that every project proposal contains a full business case, with a fully costed (i.e. Total Cost of Ownership) estimate that can stand up to independent audit, with clearly stated assumptions that can withstand rigorous analysis.
- The board must ensure that all IT-related projects are managed as part of a portfolio.
- The board must ensure that the organisation adopts and deploys a recognised project management methodology.
- The board must ensure that the organisation adopts a clearly defined, programme- and project-levels risk management plan that reflects the corporate-level risk treatment requirements.
- The monitoring framework must inform the board of progress and provide an early alert of divergence or slippage in any of the critical success factors. The board must ensure that project monitoring includes a regular, planned review of the assumptions that were fundamental to the adoption of the project in the first place.
- The board must ensure that funding is only committed on a phased basis, after conclusive verification of planned milestone achievement.
- Internal audit should be accountable directly to the board for providing regular, timely and unambiguous reports on project progress, on project slippage, budget, requirements specification and quality requirements.

Where there is project divergence, the board should not release further funds until the cause of the divergence has been fully dealt with.

Project management frameworks

The two most widely recognised and used project frameworks are:

- Project Management Body of Knowledge (PMBOK®)[66] from the US Project Management Institute (PMI).
- PRINCE2, alongside Managing Successful Programs (MSP), Management of Risk (M_o_R) and Portfolio, Programme and Project Office Guidance (P3O) from the UK's Office of Government Commerce (OGC)[67].

Both of these frameworks contain professional certifications, which enable practitioners to follow personal development paths, and organisations to identify whether or not they have adequately competent and trained resources available to meet their project management needs.

Agile project management

PRINCE2 and PMBOK projects also fail. In fact, software development has, for many years, been the area in which most projects have failed. Whether late, over budget or simply under specification, software projects have been huge value-destroyers. Not surprisingly, many software developers have been concerned about this. A key area of concern has been that projects failed because the customer

---

[66] *www.itgovernance.co.uk/pmbok.aspx.*
[67] For all of these methodologies, see *www.itgovernance.co.uk/catalog/3.*

specification either was inadequate – in which case, the developers delivered something that wasn't fit for purpose – or was so detailed, and so specific, that it was too rigid for the rapidly changing environment of the information economy and, by the time the software was completed, it was no longer what the customer wanted.

Both scenarios are also bedevilled by the widespread tendency of customers to change their minds, usually driven by a lethal combination of changing business environment, competitive pressure, improving understanding of what it is they had originally specified, and newly emergent ideas and options. Changes in project scope and requirements specification – usually in the course of a project – have always been major contributors to ultimate project disaster; few project managers have the ruthlessness and work rate that will get a complex project scoped, specified and delivered to original specification within budget, to time, and before the client changes its mind.

In the late 1990s several new ('agile') methodologies emerged, including Extreme Programming (XP), Dynamic Systems Development Method (DSDM), Scrum, Feature Driven Development (FDD), and Lean Development. Each had a different combination of old and new ideas. They were all designed for projects with tight deadlines, volatile requirements and/or emerging technologies. All focus on delivering business value, accelerating development cycles and adapting to changing business demands. They all emphasise the following factors:

- Close collaboration between the software programming team and business customers/users.
- Face-to-face communication (as more efficient than written documentation).

- Frequent (rather than once a year) delivery of new, deployable software that the business could use and would value.
- Tight, self-organising teams.
- Ways to write code that would prevent what has been seen as the 'inevitable requirements churn' from being a project crisis.

Agile development processes explicitly de-emphasise tools, but tools are nonetheless crucial to their success. Tools for software configuration management (SCM), unit testing, and software builds and build management are key to the success of agile projects. Agile teams tend to prefer open source tools and there is no standard tool set; each team must examine its particular situation and determine what tools it needs to adopt.

OPM3®

Organisational Project Management Maturity Model (OPM3®) is a relatively new standard which was published by the Project Management Institute (PMI) in December 2003. The standard is designed to provide organisations with a tool that will help them become more capable of executing their business strategies through business projects. OPM3 splits the broad concept of organisational project management into three areas for systematic management: projects, programmes, and portfolios. It recognises that organisations implement their business strategies through projects and that, therefore, project management should be a core business capability.

OPM3 is a body of knowledge about project management best practices, and this body of knowledge enables organisations to improve their current organisational project management maturity. The three interlocking elements of OPM3 (knowledge, assessment and improvement) enable organisations to assess their current state of project management maturity then map an improvement path to a higher level of maturity. Model components include best practices, capabilities, outcomes and key performance indicators.

While there may appear to be no immediate benefit in an organisation looking to OPM3 if it currently has limited or no project management methodologies in place, there is a definite long-term benefit in having a clear vision of where you want to get to in terms project management competences. Speed of implementation of OPM3 depends on the size, complexity and initial maturity of the organisation. It will also be affected by the organisation's strategic objectives, the thoroughness of the initial maturity assessment, and the level of resources that the organisation commits to the effort. Planning and implementation of OPM3 will also require significant resources. It ought to be worth investing them.

Conclusions

In the global information economy, which is characterised by information and knowledge intensity, networking, and connectivity, and in which the capture and deployment of knowledge is intrinsic to an organisation's competitive position and to its intellectual capital value, IT-supported business project execution becomes fundamental to its survival. This makes IT project governance one of the board's most important responsibilities.

CHAPTER 9: COMPONENTS OF IT GOVERNANCE

An IT governance framework consists, essentially, of a set of principles, a decision-making hierarchy and an appropriate suite of reporting and monitoring processes. While all IT governance frameworks will have common elements, few frameworks are likely to replicate one another; each organisation has a unique business model and a unique risk environment, and its IT governance framework should reflect that.

Key decision areas

There are, in fact, seven components for the corporate governance of IT that should be considered when designing an IT governance framework:

1: IT governance principles and decision-making hierarchy (see Chapter 10: ISO/IEC 38500)

There are two types of principle in this context:

- Governance principles (how IT is to be managed in the organisation).
- Implementation principles (how IT is to be used to achieve the business strategy).

2: Information strategy (see Chapter 3: Strategy: The Search for Competitive Advantage)

This must be derived from the business strategy. It deals with what information is required, where it comes from and what will be done with it.

3: IT strategy (see Chapter 3: Strategy: The Search for Competitive Advantage)

This is derived from the information strategy, and is made up of:

- IS or application strategy, which deals with how business applications and information systems are to be specified, developed, authorised, acquired, and managed.
- Architecture strategy.
- Infrastructure or technology strategy.

4: IT risk management see (see Chapter 6: Information and Continuity Risk)

Within the context of the organisation's overall enterprise risk management framework, risk to information and ICT needs to be treated in line with organisation-wide criteria. These criteria should be reflected in the controls developed as part of the IT governance framework and the reporting and monitoring processes.

5: IT architecture (see Chapter 16: Enterprise IT Architecture Committee)

This includes the integration and standardisation requirements, and must meet the requirements of the information, application and architecture strategies.

The following questions must be answered as part of developing the IT architecture:

- How are IT services (including hardware and communications protocols) specified, developed, authorised, acquired and managed?
- What services should be outsourced? How, why and to whom?

6: IT investment and project governance (see Chapter 8: Project Governance)

Given the IT strategy:

- Which IT initiatives (including outsourcing initiatives) should be implemented?
- How should they be prioritised?
- How should they be project-managed?
- What returns should be expected?
- How should the portfolio of projects be managed?
- How should any resultant business change be managed?

7: Regulatory compliance and information security (see Chapter 5: IT Regulatory Compliance)

Decisions to be made in this area are:

- What are the criteria for securing information?

- How is legal/regulatory compliance to be demonstrated?
- How should this be measured and demonstrated?
- How is intellectual property protected?
- What audits are required?

ISO/IEC 38500, the international standard for the corporate governance of information and communication technology, provides a simple and unique view of the board's role in directing, evaluating and monitoring the development and execution of IT activities in the organisation.

An IT governance framework is not a software solution, nor is there a single silver bullet that solves all of an organisation's IT governance challenges. Exactly like the corporate governance regime, the board can draw on established best practice but, ultimately, it has to develop an approach that is appropriate for its own circumstances.

CHAPTER 10: ISO/IEC 38500

This chapter describes the scope, application and objectives of ISO/IEC 38500. It also sets out some of the benefits of using the standard, in terms of the conformance and performance of the organisation. Finally, it provides a set of useful definitions, some of which are drawn from ISO Guide 73:2002 (Risk Management – Vocabulary – Guidelines for Use in Standards).

Scope

As might be expected, the scope of ISO/IEC 38500 is 'the governance of management processes (and decisions) relating to the information and communications processes used by an organization'[68]. The standard recognises that these processes could be controlled by one or more of the following:

- IT specialists within the organisation
- External service providers
- Business units within the organisation.

The standard is directed at providing 'guiding principles' for directors of organisations to help them to ensure that the use of information technology within their organisation is effective, efficient and acceptable. The standard also recognises that it has a role in providing guidance to the wide range of people whose role might be to advise, assist

---

[68] ISO/IEC 38500 Clause 1.1.

or inform directors – including external specialists and IT auditors.

Application

As is usually the case with standards published by ISO/IEC, 38500 was written to be sector-agnostic. It was designed so that it could be applied by companies of all sizes and from all sectors: public, private and not-for-profit.

Objectives

The standard aims to 'promote effective, efficient, and acceptable use of IT' in three ways:

1 By assuring stakeholders (including consumers and shareholders as well as employees and providers/vendors) that they can have confidence in the organisation's IT governance if the standard is followed.
2 By informing and guiding the directors in their IT governance activities.
3 By providing a basis for objective evaluation of IT governance. (It is this clause that is particularly interesting to IT auditors.)

Benefits

ISO/IEC 38500 'establishes a model for the governance of IT' and helps directors find an appropriate balance between risk and reward in their stewardship of the organisation's IT investment – exactly the requirement of today's corporate governance regime.

The standard identifies two principal benefits that organisations can derive from following its guidance:

1 Conformance – directors who exercise proper IT governance are more likely to address specific IT-related risks and compliance requirements (and the standard provides a series of examples of these) in a way that enables them to demonstrate that their obligations have been met.

2 Efficient management of costs – directors are not simply responsible for complying with legislation; they also have to take risks and deliver a financial return for their shareholders. In the public and not-for-profit sectors, they have to manage the costs of the organisation efficiently in order to deliver in accordance with the expectations of their various stakeholders. Directors who apply the guidance of ISO/IEC 38500 are more likely to succeed at this than those who do not. Again, the standard identifies a number of ways in which IT can contribute positively to the performance of the organisation.

Definitions

ISO/IEC 38500 contains a number of definitions of terms that are used within the standard. The terms dealing with risk are taken from ISO Guide 73:2002. The most important of these definitions is that of the corporate governance of IT, or what most people will call simply IT governance: 'The system by which the current and future use of IT is directed and controlled, Corporate Governance of IT involves evaluating and directing the use of IT to support the organisation and monitoring this use to achieve plans'. The definitions are all good, sensible, practical ones that will make sense to any director or manager and which on their own almost justify purchasing a copy of the standard!

The second chapter of ISO/IEC 38500 contains the meat of the matter, the most important part of the standard, and the core of the standard's concept of IT governance. It identifies six principles of good IT governance, and three main tasks for which directors are responsible.

The six principles of IT governance

The six principles of IT governance are intended to guide decision making, and are:

1: Responsibility

The principle of 'Responsibility' recognises that those responsible for IT within an organisation must have the authority to perform the actions for which they are responsible. The notion of accountability is contained within this principle.

2: Strategy

'Strategy' recognises that an organisation's business strategy should take into account its current and future IT capabilities; conversely, the IT strategy should reflect the requirements of the business strategy. This notion is often described as business-IT alignment – as though this is a surprising requirement!

3: Acquisition

'Acquisition' is a principle that should be applauded by stakeholders. It argues that IT investment decision-making should be clear and transparent, with an appropriate balance between cost and opportunity, a clear understanding of risk, and a view of both the short term and the long term.

4: Performance

'Performance' is one way of expressing the principle that IT should be fit for purpose.

5: Conformance

IT underpins financial accounting, and houses, supports and manipulates data on which the organisation's survival depends. The principle of 'Conformance' requires the organisation to ensure that IT complies with all regulatory and contractual requirements; standards such as ISO/IEC 27001 have a key role to play here.

6: Human behaviour

IT, of course, is part of an organisation that depends primarily on its humans; the sixth principle, 'Human behaviour', requires IT policies, practices and decisions to respect human behaviour (which is one of the terms defined in the standard).

The IT governance model in ISO/IEC38500

ISO/IEC 38500 proposes a model for IT governance, which is set out in *Figure 2* below. This model, which was first published in AS 8015:2005, is a clear and simple one that clearly contextualises the board's role in respect of IT governance.

ICT Corporate Governance

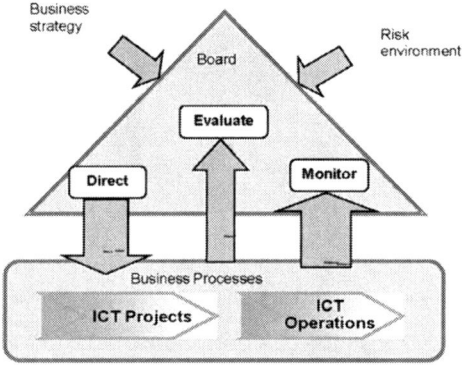

'Original image copyright ISO/IEC 2008'

Figure 2: ICT corporate governance

The standard specifies that directors must perform three main actions in respect of IT:

1 *Evaluate* the current and future use of IT.
2 *Direct* plans and policies to ensure that IT use meets business requirements.
3 *Monitor* these plans and policies to ensure that IT conforms to policies and performs in accordance with plans.

These three actions are described in detail below.

Evaluate

ISO/IEC 38500 states that directors should evaluate the current and future use of IT (including strategies, implementation plans, supply arrangements and so on, without limitation in terms of whether this is internal, external or some combination of both). Directors are encouraged to take account of pressures acting on the business, including technological change, economic and other trends, and politics; evaluations should be regular, and should be informed by and take into account current and future business needs and objectives.

Direct

The board must assign responsibility for implementation of IT plans and policies. The board, therefore, must hold management to account for delivery of those plans. Plans set out the objectives, resources and expectations for IT investment, operation and projects, while policies reflect strategic intent and provide the context for more detailed plans and should help establish sound behaviour.

This task encompasses the requirement that management supply the board with good, transparent and timely information about the progress of IT operations and projects, thus putting the board in a position to ensure that IT projects move smoothly into the operational phase without more disruption than planned for. As most IT projects fail, this aspect alone of this single IT governance action could have a significant effect on improving rates of IT project success.

Monitor

If directors want timely information that will enable them to act, they must first implement monitoring systems that will tell them what is going on – and which will alert them to any failures to comply with regulation, statute or contract. Internal audit is as much a part of effective monitoring as are clear management accountability and meaningful performance reporting.

Accountability

ISO/IEC 38500 makes a very clear statement regarding accountability: 'Accountability for the effective, efficient and acceptable use and delivery of IT by an organization remains with the directors and cannot be delegated.'

Applying the six principles

The third chapter of ISO/IEC 38500 describes how the standard's three actions intersect with the six principles; it provides guidance (summarised below) on how the six principles are to be implemented, by applying in each case the three actions. Of course, none of this is intended to be exhaustive, and each organisation is encouraged to apply 'due consideration' to its own nature and to make an 'appropriate analysis of the risk and opportunities for the use of IT'.

1: Responsibility

Evaluate:

- options for assigning responsibilities.

- the competence of those who are given operational decision-making responsibilities, with a preference for these to be business managers supported by IT specialists.

Direct:

- that plans are carried out according to assigned responsibilities.
- that required information is received.

Monitor:

- establishment of appropriate IT governance mechanisms.
- acceptance of responsibilities.
- actual performance of those who have responsibilities.

2: Strategy

Evaluate:

- developments in IT and business processes to ensure business alignment.
- IT activities to ensure improvements and developments align with changing business priorities.
- risk assessments and risk analysis to ensure that they are carried out appropriately (to appropriate international standards).

Direct:

- preparation of plans and policies that ensure organisational benefit from IT.
- a campaign to encourage submission of proposals for innovative uses of IT that enable the business to compete and perform better.

Monitor:

- progress of approved IT proposals to ensure that they achieve required objectives in required timeframes using the resources actually allocated.
- progress to ensure that IT is actually achieving 'its intended benefits'.

3: Acquisition

Evaluate:

- options for IT to realise business objectives, balancing risk, reward and value for money.

Direct:

- acquisition of appropriate IT assets – this must be suitably documented, and the organisation must have adequate capability to manage the acquired assets.
- processes to ensure that supply arrangements (internal and external) meet the organisation's supply needs.

Monitor:

- IT investments to ensure that they produce the value that was promised.
- how well members of staff – and suppliers – really understand and support the organisation's IT acquisitions.

4: Performance

Evaluate:

- management's proposed means for ensuring that IT will support business processes, with required capability and capacity, taking into account assessed risks.
- and assess risks arising from IT activities.
- and assess risks to the integrity of the information, and protection of information assets and intellectual property.
- options for assuring effective, timely decisions about the use of IT.
- (self-reflectively) the effectiveness and performance of the IT governance framework.

Direct:

- allocation of sufficient resources to ensure that IT meets its agreed objectives.
- the availability of correct, up-to-date and secure data to support the business.

Monitor:

- the extent to which IT actually does support the business.
- the extent to which prioritisation of IT resources actually matches organisational objectives.
- the extent to which IT policies are properly applied and followed.

5: Conformance

Evaluate:

- the extent to which IT meets the requirements of all applicable regulation, law, contracts and so on, and conforms with applicable policies and standards, on a regular basis.
- the extent to which the organisation conforms to its own IT governance framework.

Direct:

- IT management in establishing mechanisms and providing regular and routine reports on IT conformance with its obligations.
- the creation, maintenance and observance of policies and procedures for the correct use of IT.
- the professional development of staff, following formal professional development guidelines (i.e. certifications).
- processes to ensure that all IT actions are ethical (this is about governance, after all).

Monitor:

- to ensure that there is internal reporting and IT auditing that is timely, transparent, suitable and complete.
- all IT activities to ensure that they support the organisation in achieving its full range of obligations, ranging from data protection through to environmental impact.

6: Human behaviour

Evaluate:

- systems, processes and practices to ensure that human behaviour is allowed for (!).

Direct:

- IT activities to ensure that they are consistent with human behaviour, which should be obvious but isn't always.
- an effective IT whistle-blowing regime, such that risks or concerns from anywhere in the organisation can be drawn to the board's attention.

Monitor:

- systems, processes and practices to ensure that appropriate attention is given to human behaviour.
- systems, processes and practices to ensure that work practices are 'consistent with the appropriate use of IT'.

Alignment between ISO/IEC 38500 and the Calder-Moir Framework

The Calder-Moir IT Governance Framework is described in detail in *Chapter 12: The Calder-Moir Framework*. It is worth noting at this point that there is close alignment between the Calder-Moir Framework and the principles described in ISO/IEC 38500. The Calder-Moir Framework contains groups of IT execution processes against which the ISO/IEC 38500 principles can be mapped. Two framework process groups – IT Balance Sheet and Risk – span all six principles. The IT Balance Sheet group deals with the inventory of information and technology capabilities, and the Risk group deals with threats to those capabilities. The other groups deal with changes to, and operation of, those capabilities.

Figure 3 (below) summarises the alignment between the Calder-Moir Framework and ISO/IEC 38500.

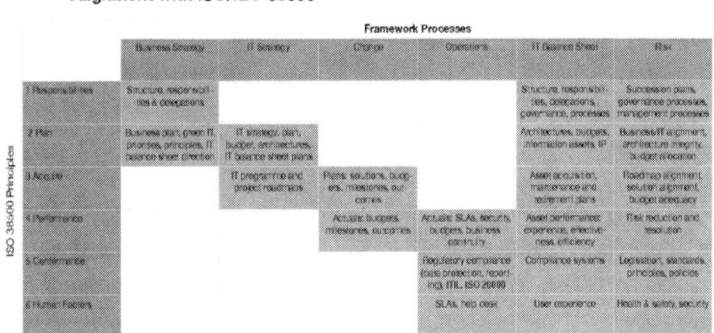

Figure 3: Alignment between ISO/IEC 38500 and the Calder-Moir Framework

CHAPTER 11: IT GOVERNANCE FRAMEWORKS AND STANDARDS

ISO/IEC 38500 is an overarching framework of principles and guidance for the directors of an organisation. It deals with the governance of IT, not its management.

A number of frameworks and standards have evolved over the last 20 years that do provide detailed guidance and support for specific areas of IT activity for which the board is responsible. Each of these frameworks has its own strengths and weaknesses, and each is capable of being used on its own or in conjunction with one or more of the other frameworks. All can be used within an ISO/IEC 38500 IT governance framework.

Frameworks

The most widely recognised frameworks which can help with both conformance and performance include:

COBIT ™

Control Objectives for Information and Related Technology (COBIT^{TM}) – is 'increasingly internationally accepted as good practice for control over information, IT and related risks. Its guidance enables an enterprise to implement effective governance over IT'[69]. This is now at release 4.1,

---

[69] www.isaca.org.

and there is a growing range of related professional qualifications[70].

ISO/IEC 27002:2005 and ISO/IEC 27001:2005

ISO/IEC 27002:2005 (previously ISO17799) is the international code of best practice for information security, and ISO/IEC 27001:2005 is the international specification against which an organisation's information security management system can be independently certified as conforming. They are also known as the BS7799 standards in the UK[71].

ISO/IEC 27005:2008 and BS3110

Two widely recognised risk management standards are ISO/IEC 27005:2008, the international code of practice for information security risk management, and BS3110, the recently launched British Risk Management Standard, whose scope is wider than just information security risk management.

Payment Card Industry Data Security Standard

Additionally, many organisations that process payment cards may have to comply with the Payment Card Industry Data Security Standard (PCI DSS)[72]. While there are few professional qualifications specifically related to PCI DSS, widely recognised information security certifications such

---

[70] See *www.itgovernance.co.uk/cobit.aspx*.
[71] See *www.itgovernance.co.uk/iso27001.aspx*.
[72] See *www.itgovernance.co.uk/pci_dss.aspx*.

as Certified Information Systems Security Professional (CISSP)[73] and Certified Information Security Manager (CISM)[74] cover much of this ground.

ITIL®

IT Infrastructure Library® (ITIL®) is an integrated set of best practice recommendations for IT service management. Although ITILv3 was released in 2007, the earlier version is still very much in use around the world[75]. There is a well-structured and comprehensive framework of professional certifications for ITIL, which is now claimed to have something in excess of 120,000 registered practitioners worldwide.

ISO/IEC 20000[76] is the associated certification standard for IT service management. It is heavily based on ITIL, and professional certifications are available.

BS25999

Business continuity management is an essential component of IT governance, just as it is an essential component of corporate governance in general. BS25999[77] is currently the world's only formal standard for business continuity management, and it provides both a specification and a code of practice that can be effectively utilised within the context of an ISO/IEC 38500 IT governance framework.

---

[73] See *www.itgovernance.co.uk/cissp.aspx.*
[74] See *www.itgovernance.co.uk/cism.aspx.*
[75] See *www.itgovernance.co.uk/itil.aspx.*
[76] See *www.itgovernance.co.uk/iso20000.aspx.*
[77] See *www.itgovernance.co.uk/BS25999.aspx.*

BS25999:2007 is also supported by more specialist standards such as ISO/IEC 24762 (the international IT disaster recovery standard) and BS25777 (the British IT Service Management Continuity Standard).

PMBoK™ and PRINCE2™

There are two main strands of project management expertise, either of which can be deployed within a project governance framework. The first is the Project Management Body of Knowledge (PMBoK™)[78], promoted by the Project Management Institute. The second is the Projects in Controlled Environments (PRINCE2™)[79] school, originated by the UK Office of Government Commerce and now incorporating Managing Successful Programmes (MSP)[80] and Management of Risk (M_o_R)[81] which, between them, provide a solid discipline for the effective management of IT projects. Both project management frameworks are supported by a structured range of professional qualifications.

The Zachman Framework and TOGAF

Enterprise IT architecture is a key part of effective IT governance and is a specialist discipline that directors may choose to consider early on. The two that are most valuable are the Zachman Framework[82] and the Open Source

---

[78] See *www.itgovernance.co.uk/pmbok.aspx*.
[79] See *www.itgovernance.co.uk/prince2.aspx* .
[80] See *www.itgovernance.co.uk/msp.aspx*.
[81] See *www.itgovernance.co.uk/M_o_R.aspx*.
[82] See *www.zifa.com*.

Architecture Framework (TOGAF)[83]. Enterprise architecture is discussed in more detail in *Chapter 16: Enterprise IT Architecture Committee.*

There is a wide range of other specialist standards and frameworks for IT management, dealing with issues ranging from capability maturity models and quality management through to procurement and operations frameworks. A comprehensive list of frameworks and associated information is available at *www.itgovernance.co.uk/frameworks.aspx.*

Conformance

Principle 5 of ISO/IEC 38500 states that directors should ensure that their use of IT meets all the requirements of applicable regulations and laws, as well as contractual obligations. The web of regulation (data protection, anti-spam, internal control, computer misuse and so on) to which an organisation may be subject is complex and ever-changing. While a number of the standards described above will help, it is important to identify the specific regulatory requirements of all those laws and regulations that might apply to the organisation, and to ensure that appropriate conformance actions are taken.

As the regulatory environment becomes more complex, it is increasingly sensible to look for some method of cross-mapping regulations to one another. The role of ISO27001 as the international standard for information security compliance has already been discussed. The best source of effective cross-mapping of IT regulatory compliance

---

[83] See *www.itgovernance.co.uk/togaf.aspx.*

requirements today is the Unified Compliance Framework (UCF)[84].

Each of the national standards or management systems deals with a different aspect of IT governance or management and each is sponsored by a different organisation. While there is often overlap between the standards, there is no single standard that on its own provides a complete IT governance framework and, of course, each sponsoring organisation has its own agenda in developing and promoting its range of standards.

Convergence

There are nevertheless growing efforts to find ways of bringing together some of these IT governance standards and frameworks. The benefits of framework integration are clear:

- Reduction in internal cost and conflict
- Increase in governance effectiveness
- Improvement in compliance
- Better alignment between the business and the IT organisation.

These efforts are, inevitably, still fragmented, not all-embracing, and are taking place at a number of levels.

COBIT-linked initiatives

The first set of initiatives is driven by ISACA and the IT Governance Institute (ITGI) and comprises a series of

---

[84]See *www.itgovernance.co.uk/ucf.aspx.*

detailed, downloadable mappings[85] between COBIT 4.1 and other standards or frameworks, including ITILv3, BS25999, Capability Maturity Model® Integration (CMMI), ISO/IEC 20000 and PMBoK®; earlier mappings, between COBIT 4.0 and PRINCE2, TOGAF 8.1 and ISO27002 are also still available. Each of these mappings is predicated on the notion that COBIT provides an overall IT governance framework, within which each of the other standards has a specific role in extending the detail and precision of COBIT. They are extremely useful for anyone looking specifically to integrate one of these standards with COBIT.

Aligning COBIT 4.1, ITILv3 and ISO/IEC 27002 for Business Benefit: A Management Briefing[86] is an attempt by the owners of two of the most widely used IT frameworks to provide a jointly authored cross-mapping that includes the international information security code of practice, and which describes how organisations can integrate these three frameworks into a single IT management system. This framework is discussed in *Chapter 18: The ITIL/COBIT/ISO27002 Joint Framework*.

Management standard convergence

Broadly speaking, management system standards are of two types:

- Specifications, which set out specifically what a particular management system must contain.

---

[85] These can all be downloaded from the IT Governance Institute website, *www.itgi.org*.
[86] This is available as free download from the websites of ITGI (*www.itgi.org*), ISACA (*www.isaca.org*), OGC (*www.ogc.gov.uk*), and TSO (*www.tso.co.uk*).

- Codes of practice, which contain a body of recognised best practice on which users can draw at their discretion.

A specification, such as ISO/IEC 27001, can be used as the basis for an audit (both internal and external), whereas a code of practice, such as ISO/IEC 27002, cannot.

There has been a significant level of convergence between management system specifications in the quality management and IT fields over the last 10 years or so. All the official standards mentioned in this article have common elements, such as use of the Plan-Do-Check-Act (PDCA) cycle, and requirements for management direction, training and awareness, monitoring and review, and so on. These common elements can be used to create an integrated management system that is also capable of audit or assessment against individual standards such as ISO/IEC 27001 or ISO/IEC 20000. PAS 99[87], from BSI, describes how these management system standards can be integrated.

There is, however, a great deal of detailed work required to integrate management systems in an effective manner. BSI is due to publish *The IT Management System of Tomorrow* in the course of 2009; this book will provide detailed guidance for organisations looking to use ISO/IEC 20000, ITIL and ISO/IEC 27001 together, and will also draw on the other frameworks and standards described in this chapter. It also provides guidance on creation of an integrated management system.

No work has yet been done to map the detailed clauses of the various business continuity standards to each other;

---

[87] See *www.itgovernance.co.uk/products/652*.

similarly, while risk management is at the heart of any governance framework, no work has yet been done to map the risk management standards to one another. Until cross-mappings emerge, organisations looking to deploy best practice in either of these areas will have to do their own preparation.

IT governance starting point

The starting point for any IT governance framework should always, of course, be the board, and ISO/IEC 38500 is the unique international standard that describes how boards should address this responsibility. As we have seen in *Chapter 10: ISO/IEC 38500*, it lays out six simple principles for 'good corporate governance of IT' and identifies the three main tasks of directors in terms of governing ICT. ISO/IEC 38500 is unique in this clear identification of the board's IT governance accountability.

End-to-end IT governance process

While ISO/IEC 38500 provides guidance for boards, it does not help organisations simultaneously to deploy any of the other standards or frameworks. The Calder-Moir IT Governance Framework does just this. It is a high-level framework that recognises each of the standards discussed in this chapter as a specific set of best practice tools, places each toolset in the context of an end-to-end process, and identifies how they can be co-ordinated to support the board, executives, and practitioners.

CHAPTER 12: THE CALDER-MOIR FRAMEWORK

The Calder-Moir IT Governance Framework[88] is a meta-model for co-ordinating frameworks and organising IT governance. It helps organisations to implement ISO/IEC 38500, the first international standard to provide guidelines for corporate governance of IT, while simultaneously drawing intelligently on all other available frameworks and standards.

IT governance is a broad subject that involves many disciplines: information technology, risk management, strategy, intellectual property, business design, project management, compliance, and so on. There are IT governance solutions and tools associated with most of these disciplines, but most of them are very detailed and have narrow scopes. No single standard, discipline or tool provides a full picture of IT governance, and collectively they can provide a confusing picture that hinders the purpose of IT governance, which is to equip boards with information and levers for directing, evaluating and monitoring IT support for their core businesses.

The Calder-Moir IT Governance Framework – originally introduced in *IT Governance Today: a Practitioner's Handbook*[89] – is not another solution, but a way of

---

[88] Copies of the white paper describing this model can be found at *www.itgovernance.co.uk/calder_moir.aspx*. The IT Governance Framework Toolkit can be purchased from *www.itgovernance.co.uk/products/519*. This toolkit is a comprehensive set of tools and templates that support the development and deployment of an IT governance framework in an organisation, using ISO38500.

[89] Alan Calder, *IT Governance Today: a Practitioner's Handbook* (ITG Publishing, 2005).

organising IT governance issues and tools to support boards, executives, and practitioners. It places IT governance tools in the context of an end-to-end process, and provides a simple reference point for discussing the many aspects of IT direction and performance.

Figure 4 below gives a graphical representation of the Calder-Moir Framework.

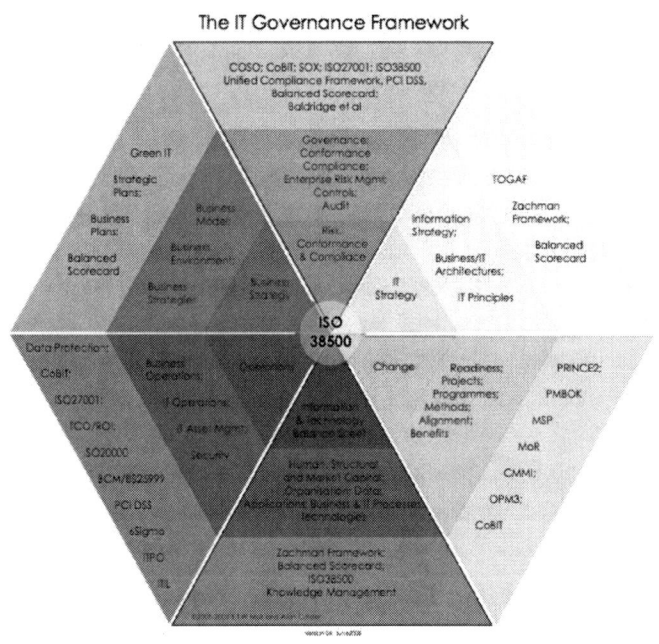

Figure 4: The Calder-Moir IT Governance Framework

The framework consists of six segments, each of which represents one step in the end-to-end process that starts with business strategy and finishes with IT operational support for delivery of business value against that strategy.

Each segment is divided into three layers:

- The innermost layer represents the board, which directs, evaluates, and monitors information technology support for business.
- The middle layer represents executive management, which is responsible for managing the activities that deliver the end-to-end process.
- The outermost layer represents the IT practitioners and IT governance practitioners, who use proven tools and methodologies to plan, design, assess, control, and deliver the IT support for business.

Navigating the framework

The top half of the framework covers the processes that establish direction, specify constraints, make decisions, and plan.

The bottom half covers the processes that develop new capabilities, manage these capabilities, and use IT to deliver business products and services.

The process starts at the '9 o'clock' position (Business Strategy), and follows the segments clockwise through the end-to-end process, as shown in *Figure 5*:

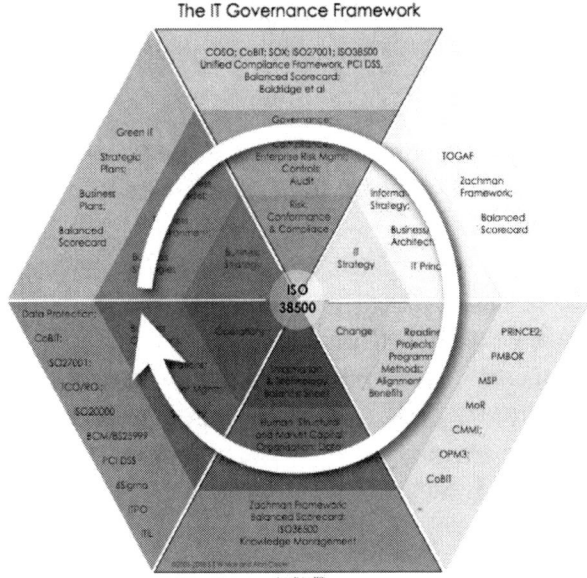

Figure 5: Navigating the Calder-Moir Framework

1: Business Strategy

The board decides the organisation's goals and business strategies. These are designed and analysed by the executive managers and their strategy practitioners. The strategies must operate within one or more corporate governance regimes (the Combined Code, Sarbanes-Oxley, Basel II, and so on).

2: Risk, Conformance and Compliance

Organisations operate within a risk environment, so it is critical to undertake a thorough risk assessment to decide which controls will be most appropriate to mitigate identified risks. The first two segments, then, describe the organisation's path and desired outcomes, the constraints within which it must operate, and the controls that will be most appropriate in those contexts.

3: IT Strategy

Once the business strategies, governance regimes, risk assessment, and controls have been developed, IT works with the business to develop architectures and plans to deliver on those requirements. The result is a set of proposals and plans that describe what business and IT should look like, the expected performance, the changes required to deliver that performance, and the resource implications. IT governance processes verify that the proposals meet the business strategy and corporate governance requirements (including risk management and controls), and help the board to evaluate the merits of the plans and proposals.

4: Change

After the board approves the plans and proposals, they can be implemented through a series of change projects. These projects are subject to regular monitoring within the IT governance regime, using controls developed in the risk assessment process.

5: Information and Technology

The change projects create or update the organisation's business and IT capabilities, which should then meet the performance and control criteria established during the planning phases.

6: Operations

These capabilities are then deployed into business and IT operations for delivery of products and services – again governed by the performance and control criteria.

Evaluate, direct, monitor

As we have seen, ISO/IEC 38500 identifies three main IT governance tasks for directors:

- Evaluate
- Direct
- Monitor.

The board evaluates the business conditions, strategies, constraints, and IT proposals. It directs by guiding the way IT should be used (according to the six principles), the appropriate risk and compliance posture, and the investment in IT proposals. And it monitors all six processes in the Calder-Moir hexagon – business strategy, business and risk environment (and constraints), IT strategy, change, capabilities, and operations. This is shown in *Figure 6* over.

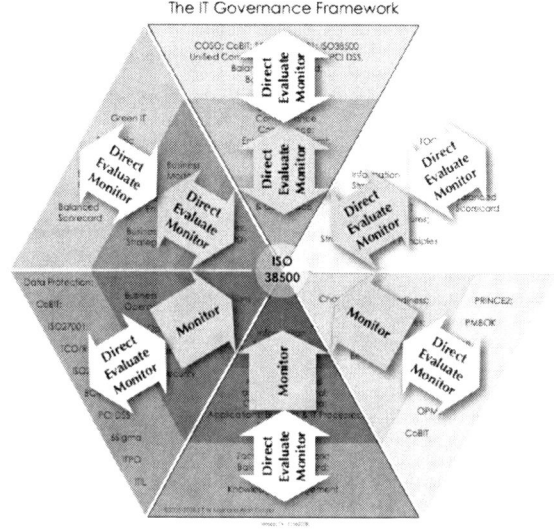

Figure 6: Evaluate, direct and monitor in the Calder-Moir Framework

If a process fails – that is, does not deliver exactly what is required – then the board intervenes (directs) through the processes in the top half of the Framework, refining or reinforcing the guidelines for business and IT.

Similarly, executive managers direct, evaluate and monitor the processes carried out by practitioners, but are – for obvious reasons – more closely involved than the directors in all activities in both halves of the framework.

Plan, Do, Check, Act

The Calder-Moir Framework is also a representation of a PDCA management cycle – Plan, Do, Check Act.

PDCA applies at two levels – a high level, reflecting the board's involvement, and a detailed level, reflecting execution of the tasks in the end-to-end process.

At a high level, the top half of the framework represents the Plan stage, and the lower half represents the Do stage. Monitoring activities in every task represent the Check stage, and feedback into the top half represents the directors' Act stage. This is shown in *Figure 7* below.

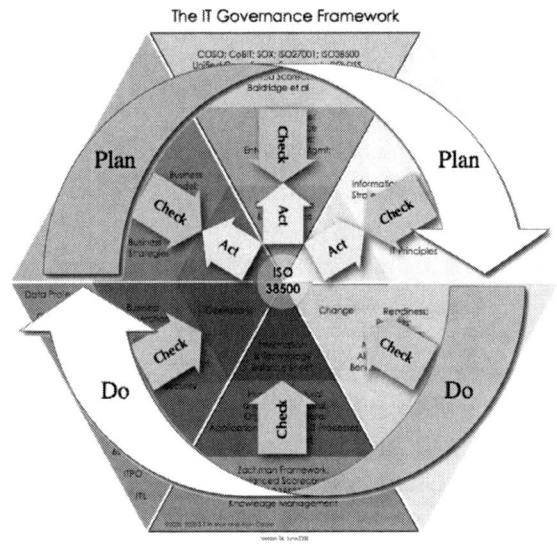

Figure 7: High level PDCA cycle

At a more detailed level, executive managers and their practitioners are interested in each of the tasks, the tools that are being used, and the outcomes that are produced at each step in the end-to-end process. The tasks within each segment should be well defined, with clear measurable objectives, management processes, and performance improvement feedback loops. This is shown in *Figure 8* below.

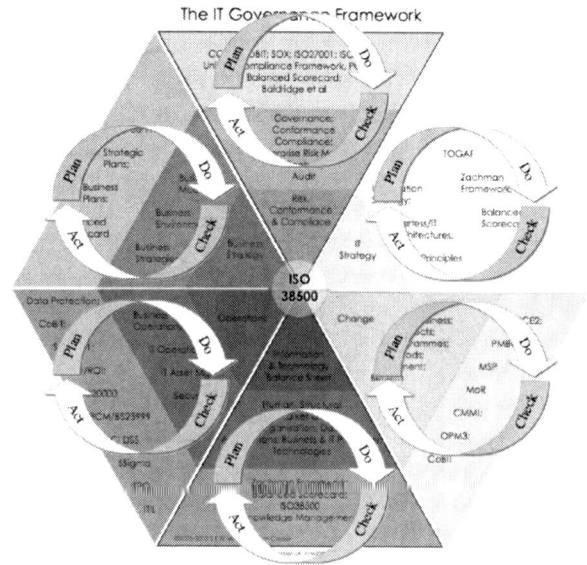

Figure 8: Detailed level PDCA cycle

Some subtleties

Finally, although it might be easy to misinterpret a meta-model such as the Calder-Moir IT Governance Framework as a rigid demarcated set of requirements, it is actually only a way of looking at the world rather than the world itself. It is worth, therefore, highlighting a small number of interactions between the segments:

- Completion of the end-to-end process – in Operations – is also the beginning of a new cycle, as actual performance is fed back into business strategy.

- Risk and compliance activities, while they initially constrain strategy, operate across all other segments in the end-to-end process.
- IT strategy and architecture activities depend on the capabilities, activities and knowledge base to develop gap analyses[90], priorities and strategies.
- Change is not only the development or acquisition of IT systems – it is also preparing and changing the business, and making sure that the change delivers the intended outcomes in operation.

---

[90] A gap analysis is an assessment of the current state of IT governance in the organisation in comparison to best practice measures.

CHAPTER 13: IMPLEMENTING IT GOVERNANCE

Implementation of an IT governance framework using the Calder-Moir Framework or any other approach is, conceptually, quite straightforward; it does, however, require substantial planning and detailed follow-through if it is to be effective. This chapter looks first at the concept of maturity models, which provide a useful context for considering how an IT governance framework may be developed and matured over time, then goes on to provide an overview of the key steps involved in implementing an IT governance framework, and finally looks at the initial issues whose resolution is essential to a successful implementation.

Maturity models

What is a maturity model?

The capability maturity model (CMM) is a useful concept for considering how best to approach IT governance. The CMM originated in the quality management sphere, as part of a framework for quality improvement, with a strong focus on process maturity. The CMM was used to describe typical organisational behaviour at each of five levels of maturity. The concept contained a strong element of evolutionary thinking, implying that an organisation evolves from a state of minimal or zero quality focus through to one where quality is an essential part of the whole organisational approach to business.

Many organisations want their business processes to become more mature on the basis that this improves their competitive capability. Maturity models provide formal roadmaps for organisations to follow in their quest to become more capable. Two of the more popular maturity models are Capability Maturity Model Integration© (CMMI©) from the US Software Engineering Institute (SEI) and the Organisational Project Management Maturity Model© (OPM3) from the Project Management Institute (PMI).

Organisations use maturity models to become more mature, or to make progress towards a 'perfected state'. Maturity models serve as reference points so that an organisation can assess itself (or be assessed by external assessors) against best practices in a particular discipline or disciplines. Maturity models typically show the capabilities of an organisation in a less mature state and the further attributes and traits of an organisation in a more mature state.

The principle is that as an organisation attains more capabilities, it becomes more mature. Some maturity models provide limited guidance on how to become more mature, and most of the content builds on itself as the users move toward higher levels of maturity. None of the many (over 30) maturity models currently in publication should be considered as methodologies or tools that organisations can start implementing the day they are purchased. An organisation must carefully analyse each model in order to understand how the model can help it to become more mature in a way that is in line with its business model and supports its business goals and strategy.

CMMI

The most comprehensive CMMI model is the CMMI for Systems Engineering/Software Engineering/Integrated Product and Process Development/Supplier Sourcing, produced by the SEI[91]. As the name suggests, this model focuses on engineering, software engineering, integrated product and process development, and supplier sourcing. It provides guidance on process management and project management, and is designed to help organisations improve their product and service development, acquisition, and maintenance processes. It may be an appropriate model for organisations that already have well-developed project management methodologies and are looking to improve, particularly if they are planning to embark on riskier, more complex projects.

The generic capability maturity model[92] has five stages. There is, of course, a pre-model stage (sometimes identified as stage zero), which describes an organisation that does not even recognise that it may have a problem, and has no discernible processes and no real interest in the matter. The five stages, for those organisations that do have an interest, are:

1: Initial: The organisation recognises that there is an issue that needs to be addressed. The processes for addressing it, however, are *ad hoc* and are applied on a case-by-case or individual basis. Management of any specific area is disorganised.

---

[91] For more information, visit the SEI website at *www.sei.cmu.edu/cmmi*.
[92] The generic maturity model described here references the one set out in detail in the COBIT management guide.

2: Repeatable: Processes have developed to the point where different people carrying out the same task apply the same procedures, but there is little or no formal training, and little or no communication of standard procedures. There is a high degree of reliance on individual skill, knowledge and application, so errors are not impossible.

3: Defined: Procedures have been defined, documented and communicated through training, but it is left to the individual to follow the procedures and, therefore, deviations may not be detected or countered. The procedures are unlikely to be anything more than a documentation of the current way of doing things.

4: Managed: At this stage, it is possible to monitor and measure compliance with the procedures and, therefore, to take action where deficiencies appear. Processes are subject to continuous improvement and now provide elements of good practice, rather than just describing actual practice. Automation and tools are beginning to be used, but not necessarily in a co-ordinated way.

5: Optimised: Processes have been refined and are now believed to represent best practice. They are based on formal continuous improvement practices and benchmarking. IT is integrated into the business, automating workflow and helping to improve quality and effectiveness.

This generic model is a useful reference point when considering IT governance implementation. COBIT has a maturity model which is very detailed and provides for the assessment of organisational process maturity for each of the 34 processes that it recognises. This is helpful in terms of producing a meaningful, objective gap analysis[93] but, as COBIT is not a complete IT governance framework, it cannot on its own provide a complete assessment. The basic concept is, however, an extremely useful one for an initial assessment of the stage of IT governance processes in an organisation.

The IT governance implementation process

This section gives an overview of the key steps involved in implementing an IT governance framework.

Pre-requisites

The two pre-requisites for the implementation of a useful IT governance framework are:

1 The board must be determined to implement – and maintain – an IT governance framework, recognising the significant benefits to the organisation, and understanding and accepting the efforts that will be required of each board member.

2 The executive and the IT governance practitioners within the organisation must commit themselves whole-heartedly to designing and delivering an IT governance framework that will meet the board's requirements.

Given these pre-requisites, the implementation process has two, ultimately convergent strands.

---

[93] An assessment of the current state of IT governance in the organisation in comparison to best practice measures.

Strand 1

The first strand is the performance of a gap analysis and the development of a plan that will close the gap. It consists of the following tasks:

- Self-assessment of IT governance practices in the organisation.
- Identification of, and agreement upon, the size of the gap that is to be closed.
- Prioritisation (and datelining) of focus areas.
- Delegation of responsibilities.
- Authorisation of adequate resources.
- Monitoring, review and management.

Strand 2

The second strand is an identification of what the business strategy specifically requires of the IT infrastructure and the IT team, and the development of a plan to deliver it. It consists of the following tasks:

- Clarification of business strategy.
- Identification of key competences and key intellectual assets.
- Creation/confirmation of risk management framework.
- Identification of required applications and ICT strategy.
- Comparison to the ICT infrastructure actually deployed and services available.
- Prioritisation (and datelining) of areas for change.
- Delegation of responsibilities; starting to integrate these with strand 1 responsibilities.
- Authorisation of adequate resources; starting to integrate these with Strand 1 responsibilities.

- Monitoring, review and management; starting to integrate these with Strand 1 processes.

These two strands must ultimately become one; the organisation's governance structures must ensure that the IT team delivers an IT infrastructure that meets – and goes on meeting – the organisation's strategic goals within the context of its risk treatment plan.

Initial completion

The final stage of the implementation process is reached when the governance structure that has been implemented is firmly in control of the IT infrastructure, and the organisation as a whole understands and is benefiting from the strategic and operational alignment of IT with the organisation and its goals. From this point forward, the board and executive governance mechanisms should be adequate to ensure that the organisation/IT alignment continues and that the business increasingly benefits from its IT infrastructure. This future process can include deployment of more sophisticated IT optimisation tools.

Issues that must be resolved

This section discusses the initial issues whose resolution is essential to a successful implementation.

The problem of silo management

Most organisations are vertically structured. They are made up of a collection of pyramids, each reporting to a senior leader (CFO, line of business head, sales director, territory director, etc.). Each has well-established lines of communication between the base and the apex. Information is similarly held and channelled within 'information silos' – vertically separate stacks of deep, tightly matted undergrowths of hardware, operating systems, applications, customisation, information, use, practice and (sometimes) culture.

As a result, most organisations are, in effect, vertically disintegrated. They have also, over the last 10 years, tended to pursue software automation projects on a silo-by-silo basis. Where these projects have been successful, they have usually also automated this vertical disintegration; the various technologies deployed are not often compatible and, even if they were, the information processed is often slightly different (sometimes merely in terms of ratio definition) from business unit to business unit, even though the underlying facts are the same.

This situation is exacerbated in organisations built on merger and acquisition activity. Most of these organisations have (to some extent) justified the investment with proposed head office and administration cost savings that presuppose a level of infrastructure integration capability that simply doesn't exist. This results in scenarios such as the large financial institution that runs multiple types of operating systems, multiple applications and multiple hardware specifications (of differing ages and upgrade potential), all within the same high-rise building. These organisations have what might be called an institutional information dis-integration strategy

At the same time as organisations have been embedding their silo management philosophies, they have also been attempting to respond to a wave of technological innovation, often involving e-commerce and the Internet, usually in order to be agile and more effective and sometimes simply to keep up with sector leaders. As a result, most organisations have imposed several layers of technology on top of their vertically dis-integrated information models. (This is a major part of the reason why large organisations have to have a hand-cranked vulnerability patching procedure, and why business process software such as SAP, which works across a number of individual silos, often has to have a lot of expensive, non-upgradeable customisation.)

These silos exist because of the historical absence of an IT governance framework. Implementation of a meaningful IT governance framework will lead the organisation into the sunny uplands of IT that is fit for business purpose – but this journey will involve an extensive weeding exercise and a Herculean cleaning task.

This inevitably means expense, of two kinds. Firstly, it is necessary to write off useless or redundant hardware and software and replace it with fit-for-purpose alternatives. Secondly, there is the possible expense of replacing a number of the people whose commitment to and passion for the *status quo ante* leaves them unable to participate enthusiastically in the future. Of course, the cleaning, weeding, and re-planting processes will themselves require a substantial commitment of resource and effort.

In other words, do not embark on an IT governance programme lightly. Plan it carefully, resource it properly, quantify the expected benefits clearly, and manage it ruthlessly. Success may require several years of sustained effort.

Pursuit of this objective, the implementation of a complete, working IT governance framework, cannot occur in a vacuum. The organisation has to continue competing, which means evolving and adapting to the changing business environment. This means that the outline IT governance framework should be erected and working early, clear guidelines should be established and deployed, and there should be a clear delineation between strategic business technology goals and short-term, tactical IT objectives. In other words, the organisation should avoid signing up for any of those long-term technology projects that end up delivering something that is no longer required.

Obtaining the board's buy-in

The first of the preliminary steps identified earlier was obtaining the board's buy-in. Of course, it must be more than buy-in, as IT governance is about the board taking direct ownership of, and responsibility for, governing IT in the organisation. Boards tend, however, to focus only on the issues they believe are crucial for the organisation's success and, as a result, they often will not allow IT governance onto the agenda unless one or more of the board members insist on it. Ideally, the Chairperson or CEO should be the person behind the IT governance initiative – if it is anyone else, the project may well be downplayed, downgraded and deflected from.

Of course, all organisations actually do have an approach to governing IT; it is just not always a satisfactory one. In many organisations, the approach is one of abdication. Custom and practice dictate that IT investment guidelines allow any IT investment that the business says it wants. IT project returns on investment (ROI) go unmeasured, incompatible software and hardware is purchased in the belief that custom joins will provide the best of all worlds, and it is accepted that when the going gets tough, the IT budget gets cut. This is reminiscent of attitudes to marketing, another business area that has not always been too hot on delivering quantifiable, fit-for-purpose solutions which provide, in times of trouble, proven models for reliably generating proven returns.

So, given that all organisations already have an IT governance framework of a sort, what this book is talking about is the process of turning it into a good one, an effective one; one that adds value to the organisation, reduces cost, and improves measurability and compliance, while reducing risk and improving competitiveness. To do this, the board has to own the initiative.

How do you get their buy-in? If they are simply not interested, you can't. However, the senior non-executive director and/or the audit committee usually have enough embedded authority – and a relevant context – to push it firmly up the board agenda. The argument for IT governance is clearly laid out in *IT Governance: Guidelines for Directors*[94]; board members – including the non-executives, and particularly the senior non-executive and those on the audit committee – should be encouraged to read it, to help them develop their awareness and move them through appreciation and concern to understanding and action.

---

[94] Alan Calder, *IT Governance: Guidelines for Directors* (ITGP, 2005), available at *www.itgovernance.co.uk/products/19*.

Identify symptoms

At the heart of any director's successful effort to get IT governance onto the board agenda are an enquiring mind, a strong streak of common sense, and a determination to leverage IT and the organisation's intellectual assets for the long-term benefit of the organisation and all its stakeholders – particularly the shareholders. There is often a handful of key questions whose answers are fundamental to what the organisation needs to change in terms of its IT governance. Here are eight questions for the board that will help identify symptoms of inadequate IT governance:

1 How does your board assess (measure) the real contribution made by any of your IT systems to improving the organisation's competitiveness?

2 On the subject of the benefits of IT systems and projects, what divergence is there between the views of your sales/operational management and those of your IT management? Who is right and how do you find out? Are you getting maximum value (maximum business benefit for minimum actual total cost) for each of your IT investments? How would you know? How would you know if your IT spend is putting your company at a cost disadvantage?

3 What is your board's process for comparing the (fully TCO-costed) ROI on your technology projects to those of any other strategic options, including acquisitions, and how does this affect strategic planning?

4 What is your board's view on the relationship, in your organisation, between the potential impact of a compliance or information security failure (in financial terms) and the (fully absorbed) cost of meeting the compliance and security objectives? What is the total actual (direct and indirect) cost of all the compliance and

information security incidents in your organisation in the last twelve months?

5   What is the real, financial value to your organisation of its information and intellectual capital and how are you leveraging it?

6   How are you driving up the intellectual capital/headcount ratio? What is the relationship between this ratio and the IT intensity (IT investment to headcount) ratio?

7   Do all your IT projects come in on time, to budget and to specification?

8   How does your Directors and Officers Liability Insurance (D&O) deal with the personal consequences for directors of IT failures arising from inadequate board oversight of core business processes and significant financial transactions?

Some of these questions may have an immediate resonance within organisations that do not already have an established IT governance framework. They will resonate because the organisation has a history of poor IT project delivery, because applications are not felt to be fit for purpose, because the organisation is being out-competed by one or more rivals who are making better use of technology, or because there have been significant information security or compliance issues either inside the company or in other companies in the sector.

The IT governance practitioner will therefore identify and target these two or three key corporate issues and ensure that the broader questions are asked determinedly – preferably with some reference to how things appear to be done differently elsewhere, with different (better) results. Like any good bridgehead, these questions enable one to explore other areas, until the underlying need for an IT governance framework is laid bare. Some organisations may choose to bring in outside consultants to do this but, apart from the usual benefit of getting a third party to tell your people what you already know, there is no good commercial reason to pay good money to an outside firm for doing something you can do perfectly well yourself.

Organisational politics and IT governance

Of course, this can be an intensely political process. Implementation of an IT governance framework involves the transfer, from an incumbent technology chief to the board, of significant strategic influence and ultimate power over very substantial budgets and sometimes large specialist teams (for good or, quite often, for worse). While it is sometimes true that the technology chief (CIO, CTO, or similar title) will wholeheartedly support such a re-alignment, recognising the importance to the business of an IT governance structure, it is possible that this transfer of power will be fiercely resisted.

This resistance may well include an attempt to turn IT governance into an essentially IT-driven activity, or to otherwise undermine and divert the strategy and its implementation. There are already a number of vendors happy to collaborate in positioning IT governance as an IT organisation initiative, one that primarily involves the purchase of some specialist software to be used by the IT organisation, perhaps to provide the board with information of some sort.

IT governance is not an IT-driven activity. It is the board's responsibility to ensure that its investments in IT deliver, for the business, the strategic value that is required, and that the real IT-related operational risks that the organisation faces are properly and effectively dealt with.

Sometimes, the need to first complete an existing project (such as Sarbanes-Oxley section 404 compliance, an IFRS application rollout, or a major upgrade or business-specified application development) is cited as a practical reason to defer starting an IT governance effort 'just yet'; once the project is out in the long grass it will, with a bit of determination, stay there.

Of course, there may well be a number of board members who simply do not want to have to deal with IT. (This might include the members who are still proud of not having a computer on their desks, or who have their e-mails printed out so that they can read them.) These individuals are likely to resist creation of an IT governance framework. The board, though, has to be onside; this is why the chairman, the CEO, the senior non-executive and the audit committee can all make such a huge contribution to getting the board to focus on the need properly to govern IT.

Implementation of an IT governance framework, then, will clearly be an intensely political and risky process. It is even harder in the public sector than in the private, and this reflects the very different public-sector drivers of IT projects. Public-sector IT projects would not destroy so much value if they were better governed. For this to happen, though, the boards responsible for overseeing them would have to be very focused and determined in establishing, implementing and maintaining workable IT governance mechanisms – sometimes in the face of fierce resistance from their central paymasters ('Very brave, Chairman, very brave – but I'm not sure the Minister will appreciate delays in delivering a manifesto commitment').

Conclusions

The IT governance practitioner has the hard task of attempting to create the necessary environment for an IT governance framework to be established and become successful. Frankly, any attempt to push forward with an IT governance strategy that does not have the board's determined support (including, at the least, that of the chairman, the CEO and either the audit committee or the senior non-executive director) is doomed to failure. It would be better to continue working to get their commitment to the concept than to embark, ill-supported, on a project whose inevitable (either partial or complete) failure will be quietly cheered as evidence that 'IT governance is just another one of those fads'.

It isn't.

CHAPTER 14: DECISION MAKING AND THE IT ORGANISATION

The two executive roles that are critical to the effective implementation of an IT governance framework are those of the CEO and the CIO. Both roles have existed for some time, and the relationship between the two is not always a successful one. We think that any IT governance initiative will fail if the organisation does not appoint a CIO to a role that has adequate authority and scope for effective IT management. It will also fail if it does not have the complete support of the board and the CEO.

There are a number of other roles – such as Chief Technology Officer (CTO), Chief Knowledge Officer (CKO), Chief Information Security Officer (CISO), Chief Security Officer (CSO), and Chief Privacy Officer (CPO) – and a number of key IT functions – development (and engineering), innovation, integration, support, training, network/infrastructure management, information security, compliance, etc. – that need to be addressed in a coherent way at the same time as clearly establishing the CIO role. The CIO also has other critical internal relationships – with the Chief Financial Officer (CFO), the Chief Operations Officer (COO), the Chief Compliance Officer (CCO), the business line managers, logistics, sales and marketing people, and the procurement staff.

The starting point is the governance one: 'corporate governance is the system by which business corporations are directed and controlled'[95]. Another simple definition of IT governance, therefore, is 'the system by which IT organisations are directed and controlled'. Getting IT governance right clearly depends on getting the management structure right.

If IT is fundamental to the information economy, if most organisations depend on information technology, and if information technology budgets are a substantial and critical part of both the annual cost and the investment budget, then the IT leadership and the IT team are at least as important to the organisation's future as the business unit leadership and the business unit teams. In some industry sectors – like finance and banking, and any organisation with a significant online sales channel – the IT team may even be more important than the business unit teams.

The CEO

The CEO is responsible for actually making IT governance work in the organisation. The board has to determine strategic goals and key IT principles. The board has to mandate the creation of an appropriate IT governance structure, and commit itself to acquiring the knowledge and expertise to contribute to and monitor the deployment and use of IT in the organisation in line with the business requirements. But it is the CEO who has to make this happen. This means that the CEO simply has no option but to become sufficiently knowledgeable about the strategic IT governance and business issues to ensure that IT makes the quality of contribution that it should. If IT fails to deliver,

---

[95] *OECD Principles of Corporate Governance,* 1999.

the first person who should be accountable for the failure is the CEO.

'Does IT matter?'[96] 'Is IT still capable of being a strategic differentiator for us?' 'Is someone out there preparing a technology silver bullet for us?' 'Are we really leveraging our intellectual assets to their fullest extent?' 'Am I likely to go to jail?'

These are key question for CEOs of all organisations, key questions that cannot even be considered, let alone answered, without having first got to grips with the subject – not at the detailed, bits and bytes level, but at the strategic, business, social and economic levels. Answering these questions means that the CEO must either be a visionary technologist – or have on the executive team someone who is not only a visionary technologist but who is also able to help develop and then execute the organisation's IT strategy.

The CEO has to step beyond seeing the CIO simply as the expert in technology and service delivery, and instead see him or her as an essential component of the top management team. The CEO must first appoint an IT leader who will ensure that the IT unit adds real value to the organisation, and then structure the organisation so that the CIO is part of the top executive management team, with equal status to the CFO, the COO and other similar roles. Strategic planning without the involvement of the CFO, COO or business area leaders (or equivalents) is inconceivable; it should be equally inconceivable without the CIO being involved on precisely the same basis as the

---

[96] For a discussion of this question, see Nicholas G. Carr, *Does IT Matter? Information Technology and the Corrosion of Competitive Advantage* (HBS Press, 2005).

other business executives. The CIO has to be as close an advisor to and decision-maker for the CEO as are the CFO and the handful of other top executives in the organisation.

The CEO has to ensure that the development of the information strategy, the IT strategy and the IT goals takes place amongst the top team, working together. The CEO therefore has to ensure that business executives and technology experts are able to talk a common language and share a common goal – and that these goals translate into clearly articulated IT targets and performance metrics (in just the way, for instance, that the goals of HR, sales or operations do) that relate to the shared perception of how IT performance will contribute to the organisation's overall strategic success.

Finally, the CEO has to get the organisation behind the business vision for information and IT, ensuring that line of business managers and users everywhere understand – through a realistic, hype-free internal communication strategy – what is expected of IT, the contribution that IT is going to make to the business in the future, and what is expected of the users of IT.

The CEO should be clear that business unit leaders are expected to work with the CIO intelligently to define technology requirements at the user level, and that the CIO is expected to work with the business heads to deliver, implement and get full value out of every new technology initiative. In other words, the business culture has to exclude the more common situation in which the technology people develop a system and then hand it over to the business to deploy and moan about; both sides of the organisation have to be fully involved in both phases of the project. When that happens as a matter of course, IT is an integral part of the business.

The CIO

The CIO, like the CFO, should be one of the organisation's inner executive cabinet. Ideally, it should be someone with a width of business experience (including, perhaps, a good MBA) and a depth of technology experience (including a first degree in computing and practical, relevant experience in the key IT disciplines: programme management, performance optimisation, security, compliance, enterprise IT architecture).

The CIO needs to be a leader more than a technology specialist, and must have the competence to structure the IT organisation in such a way that it will deliver the IT strategic goals. This means recruiting and retaining, at all levels of the IT organisation, staff that have the right mix of technical and business skills to deliver the required IT performance within the broader organisational culture. And these skills are as much about relationship-building, responsiveness, service and performance orientation, and results focus as they are about protocols, network layers and service stacks.

The CIO has to fight for, and win, an operational unit budget that will allow the creation of an IT organisation that is genuinely fit for purpose, the purpose being the delivery of the organisation's strategic business goals. This may also require dedicated resource: HR staff, for instance, who understand the skill sets and competences required for staff in the IT organisation.

The CIO also has to manage communication between the IT team and the rest of the organisation, building a sense of shared commitment to the organisation's goals. At the same time, the CIO has to ensure that users throughout the organisation understand – in a realistic, hype-free manner – the IT unit's objectives and plans.

The CIO: role description

The CIO has two main objectives:

- To ensure that the organisation's IT team and ICT infrastructure support its business goals and reflect the key IT implementation principles determined by the board.
- To ensure that the organisation's business and information strategies leverage as completely as possible its intellectual assets and ICT infrastructure, taking account of relevant technology changes and developments in the business environment.

In order to achieve these objectives, the scope of the CIO's responsibilities should encompass, but not be limited to, all of the organisation's information and information-related activities, which include:

- desktop and enterprise systems
- network and telecommunications services
- hardware
- software
- data administration
- publishing
- libraries (if they exist)
- archives and records management.

The CIO must also be responsible for the specification, development, and deployment of systems, project- and contract-management, and information-related procurement. The significant compliance and security aspect of information means that information security, regulatory compliance and privacy should also be within the CIO's scope. All of this has clear implications for the organisational reporting hierarchy, to which we will return below.

The CIO must be accountable for planning and managing all of the organisation's information and ICT resources to support business unit managers in successfully pursuing their business objectives. He or she must also provide intelligent and informed executive-level support for and input into the organisation's strategic business, information and financial planning activities. The direct, executive accountability for the successful alignment of the IT unit and all of the organisation's information and ICT assets with the business should sit squarely and uncompromisingly with the CIO.

Key CIO challenges

The CIO has to structure the functions – and therefore the management team – of the IT unit to take account of the core competences that the IT team needs to retain (or develop) and those which could be more cost-effectively outsourced. Below are a number of key strategic business issues that the CIO needs to address.

Culture

The CIO is responsible for developing the internal culture of the IT unit within the organisation. Organisational culture is the product of a set of values expressed through a number of activities over a period of time. The CIO has to develop – within the culture of the organisation as a whole – an IT organisation culture that will ensure that the IT team contributes to ultimate organisational success. While every CIO will have specific views, and every organisation will impose particular restraints, many of the essential characteristics of an IT unit's culture are summed up by the phrase 'a pragmatic, can-do business attitude'. A cost-conscious, practical IT unit that is focused on delivering systems and services that are fit for purpose, which will help the organisation achieve its business goals, and which will usually perform better than promised ('under promise, over deliver') is an IT unit that will be successful.

Innovation

In the information economy, where technology can give organisations a significant edge, the CIO needs to explore ways in which current or evolving technology can be deployed to the organisation's advantage. This includes identifying ways in which technology can improve information availability, reduce costs, and improve business processes and service delivery.

Asset leverage

An organisation possesses significant intellectual assets; the CIO has to ensure that those assets are all identified and appropriately valued, and that plans to exploit them (within the overall context of the business strategy and goals) are developed and implemented. This does not mean that the CIO should initiate business activities that, although they might exploit existing assets, are not part of the business strategy. Rather, those assets that cannot be exploited should be sold to generate funds that can then be invested in other, more productive assets.

The CIO also needs to ensure that, at all levels of the organisation, the value of information as an asset is understood. If information is the lifeblood of the twenty-first century organisation, everyone in the organisation has to know what is required, why it is required, how to collect it and how to safeguard it. In addition, the CIO needs to ensure (alongside the business heads and functional specialists such as HR and training) that, throughout the organisation, there are sufficient skills and competences for users to take full advantage of the information assets that are available.

Strategy

The CIO has to help develop, and then drive implementation of, the information strategy, creating a coherent ICT plan, and an enterprise IT architecture that meets the board's requirements and is appropriate for both the near- and long-term needs of the organisation.

Operations

The CIO has to ensure that day-to-day IT operations (network activity, applications, hardware, communications, help desk, etc.) all operate effectively, smoothly, and seamlessly, so that the users' experience of IT is that it enables them to succeed at their jobs. The CIO also needs to ensure that meaningful metrics are established and that an appropriate IT performance monitoring system (such as the IT Balanced Scorecard) is developed and deployed and that, throughout the organisation, it is widely understood that the IT unit has to deliver objective, meaningful results in just the same way as every other functional and operational unit.

Staffing

The CIO has to ensure that the IT unit is adequately staffed, and that there is an appropriate mix of technical, inter-personal and business skills that will enable the unit to deliver the quality and level of service required of it. Succession planning, recruitment and training are all key areas.

Processes and quality

ICT has a specific role to play in process automation and in business and service quality. The CIO has to ensure that the IT unit develops and promotes effective and efficient business-oriented processes in relation to information-gathering and -dissemination, ensuring that systems are improved and developed in line with process and quality improvements.

Compliance and security

The CIO has to ensure that the organisation complies (on an agreed basis) with the host of regulations and statutes in all the jurisdictions in which the organisation has operations, particularly those relating to data protection, privacy, intellectual property rights (IPR) protection and computer misuse. Similarly, the CIO has to ensure that appropriate arrangements are made to protect all of the organisation's information assets, to recover from business interruptions and to maintain business continuity when disaster strikes.

IT management structure

As will be clear from the foregoing, our view is that the CIO is where the buck stops for everything to do with the organisation's information assets and ITC infrastructure, and that the CIO is accountable for helping develop and then execute the information and dependent strategies. It follows from this that all information-related activity, all information-related roles, teams and functions, and all information-related budgets, should come within the CIO's area of responsibility.

In the twenty-first century, the key functional areas for the CIO's department are:

- Asset exploitation and innovation – the identification and exploitation of the organisation's information and intellectual assets, which include data storage, data mining, and knowledge deployment (for example, intranets, business intelligence, groupware).
- Technology – the specification and development of technologies that meet the business need, and which therefore logically include the enterprise IT architecture and the organisation's ICT infrastructure.
- IT services – including network management, enterprise systems (ERP, CRM, supply chain management, etc.), operations, support and system deployment.

- Information security, privacy and compliance.
- Project management – this sits across the top of all the other activities and has to be part of the wider organisational approach to project management. Note that the organisation's programme office should not usually report to the CIO; its cross-organisational importance and the need for segregation of duties both suggest that it should report either to a COO or to the CFO – and sometimes to the CEO.

Reporting to the CIO, the IT unit's management team should (depending on the size of the organisation and its particular competitive positioning) therefore consist of:

- the Chief Knowledge Officer, responsible for exploiting the organisation's information assets.
- the CTO, responsible for technology development.
- a Chief IT Operations Officer, responsible for the whole range of IT services and user support.
- the CISO, responsible for information security and compliance.

If the organisation has a Chief Security Officer (or equivalent, responsible primarily for physical security), then this role should report to the CISO – physical and logical security management simply has to be integrated[97], otherwise physical intruders can find themselves in a position to do logical damage that the organisation cannot afford. Clearly, the CISO will also need to have a good working relationship with the internal HR team and the organisation's legal advisers.

---

[97] See Alan Calder and Steve Watkins, *IT Governance: a Manager's Guide to Data Security and ISO27001/ISO27002* (Kogan Page, 2008).

IT organisational structure

In a large, complex organisation, the IT management structure will probably look something like this:

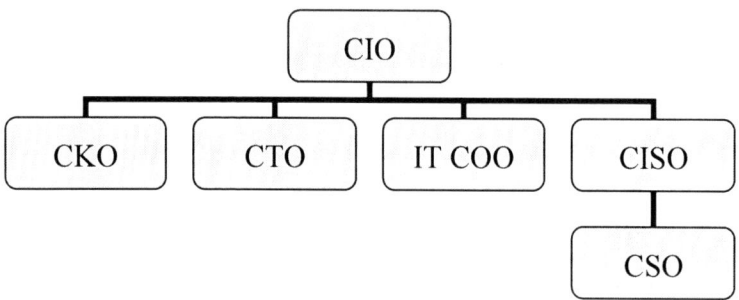

Figure 9: IT organisational structure

All of these executives will need to have effective working relationships with the internal procurement team, the enterprise risk management team, the finance team and, of course, the business teams who depend on them for success in the marketplace. The intelligent CFO will also embed one or more finance people in the IT team (and certainly within projects) to ensure that all financial issues are correctly understood and recorded.

In addition, there may be IT management structures in subsidiary companies or divisions, depending on the organisational culture and information strategy. The way those subsidiary management structures are designed will be dependent on the organisation itself, but they should *a)* be capable of plugging into a central structure not dissimilar to the one above, and *b)* have very strong cross-functional and inter-organisational linkages built into them. It is, after all, essential that the IT team – at all levels – lives and breathes the sense of integrated, joined-up commitment it is seeking with the business.

Outsourcing

A key strategic option for all businesses is outsourcing[98] functions and services that may have become commoditised, or that are not seen as core to the organisation's strategic success[99]. Every organisation will have its own definition of core competence, and the core competences of the IT unit – both those that exist and those that are required – should be identified early on. Outsourcing options should only be considered in the context of the business model, strategy and objectives, and in relation to required core competences. It is essential that the assessment of core and non-core competences pays extremely careful attention to what the business may require in a number of years' time; outsourcing something that does not look important today will turn out to have been an expensive error when it has to be insourced in a few years' time, when its criticality to the future strategy has been belatedly recognised.

There is often a strong argument for looking at outsourcing a wide range of support services; this industry is already well developed. There are equally strong arguments for

---

[98] 'Outsourcing' is not synonymous with 'offshoring'. The geographical location of an outsourcing company is an issue to take into account, but whether or not to outsource is a business imperative.

[99] The fact that many organisations have discovered that their outsourcing decisions were wrong, and now have to insource the operation so recently and so painfully outsourced, is of course not a negative comment on outsourcing itself, but rather on the managements concerned.

outsourcing a number of other functions. The financial benefits that might be derived from outsourcing, while important and possibly significantly large, should not be the primary driver in considering the outsourcing option. The primary driver should be strategic; in other words, the organisation should have a strategic approach to outsourcing, in the light of which it should carry out its assessment of the benefits of outsourcing individual activities and functions.

Outsourcing is not the right solution for a management problem (such as 'why is the system down again?'), nor is it a reliable way of getting better management into something that is currently poorly managed (how will you determine what service you require from an outsourcing partner if you don't know how to do it yourself?), and it is certainly not the same as offshoring or relocating a function that you continue to operate yourself. Every option has to be considered as carefully, as ruthlessly and as systematically as for any other investment project.

Supplier selection

A well-informed strategic decision to outsource services that are not seen as core, either today or in the long term, must also be well executed, otherwise the organisation will suffer operational cost, customer damage and regulatory exposure. The board must be satisfied that the organisation is capable of selecting suppliers of outsourced services, taking into account the following requirements:

- The supplier must be able to provide the required services to the required standard. This means it must be adequately resourced, managed and capitalised, and must have a reputation and referees, and perhaps external standard certifications (such as ISO20000), that demonstrate this capability.

- There must be strategic alignment and cultural fit between the buyer of the services and their supplier; in other words, they are both likely to benefit (other than financially) from the relationship.
- The cost/benefit ratio must make real sense, remembering that the supplier is in it to make money too.
- All of the legal and compliance issues, particularly around information security and privacy, must be adequately dealt with. (This makes any outsourcing partner's ISO27001 certification a practical prerequisite.)

The outsourcing organisation should appoint a senior manager to be responsible for evaluating suppliers against their capacity to meet the broad range of organisational policy and legal requirements. As well as ensuring that there is detailed financial and legal due diligence, this manager must:

- evaluate the supplier's track record and reputation; look at any complaints and attempt to identify patterns that can be traced back to other activities controlled by the supplier.
- evaluate the supplier's location, corporate ICT infrastructure and national backbone, looking for issues that might affect continuity or quality of service; carry out site visits and, if necessary, independent audits (e.g. SAS 70).
- consider local cultural and ethical issues that may reduce the level of care for customer and employee information.

- tell customers, in good faith, what he intends to do; identify possible risks, and tell them how to deal with any eventualities – a customer forewarned may well be a customer retained!
- ensure that the supplier performs background checks on, and effectively supervises, its employees and other contractors.
- ensure that the supplier has an effective means of communicating with its customers about security, privacy and business continuity breaches immediately they occur.

Outsourcing contracts

An outsourcing relationship might be expected to endure for a considerable period. The relationship should therefore be thought through in great detail before contracts are finalised. ISO27002 provides detailed guidance on a number of the issues that should be dealt with in any outsourcing contract[100]. The contract should:

- give a clear description of services to be provided, in order to avoid later questions about what services are in scope, what are not, and what constitute a contractual change that incurs extra fees.
- clarify the extent to which the customer will have input into how the services it is buying are performed.
- require the supplier to change the services to keep pace with technological advances. There should also be a

---

[100] See also Alan Calder and Steve Watkins, *IT Governance: a Manager's Guide to Data Security and ISO27001/ISO27002* (Kogan Page, 2008) for extensive, detailed advice about outsourcing contracts.

requirement that performance improve over time, as the supplier's experience increases and economies of scale kick in; and there should be a procedure for benchmarking the supplier's services against improving industry standards.

- provide, if applicable, for the performance of an SAS 70 review on at least an annual basis. This applies to any organisation subject to Sarbanes-Oxley, which may, when assessing its own financial controls, have to consider the extent to which any of its outsourced service providers fall within the scope of its control assessment.
- clarify which party owns work performed, or intellectual assets created, by the supplier on behalf of the customer during the period of the contract.
- give the customer a right to terminate the contract at its convenience, although there will usually be a termination fee to pay.
- clearly describe how responsibilities are divided between the supplier and the customer. Usually, the supplier will have primary responsibility for the performance of specific tasks and processes identified in the contract, and the customer will have a right to give input and approval.
- provide for sharing cost savings between the supplier and the customer, as well as bonuses if the supplier significantly exceeds service levels.
- be particularly clear as to which party is responsible for the costs of compliance with new laws and obtaining, where required, licences.
- include provisions for regular performance review, dispute escalation, and non-legal settlement of disputes.

All organisations that outsource significant activities have to grapple with the strategic dilemma of whether they concentrate on building deep, long-lasting relationships with a small number of strategic suppliers, or whether they manage a portfolio of outsourcing suppliers, each of whom are given some part of the business. The latter option can be an effective way of splitting the risks (such as supplier failure, service deterioration, price inflation); it does, however, have its own specific costs and disadvantages. Each organisation has to go with the solution that is appropriate to its own circumstances.

CHAPTER 15: IT STEERING COMMITTEE AND EXECUTIVE COMMITTEE

The two key layers of any IT governance framework are a board-level IT steering or strategy committee and a management-level executive committee. This chapter explores both types of committee.

IT steering committee

The board needs to create a mechanism – the IT steering committee – through which it can provide the business with strategic technology leadership. Technology/IT leadership requires a specific mechanism, in a way that HR, Sales or Marketing, for example, do not. These other divisions are usually already effectively dealt with as part of the existing board agenda; most board members already understand the issues around sales and marketing, and the people involved in making sales happen already get a great deal of informed attention. The organisation almost certainly already has well-developed governance frameworks for these key activities. No additional benefits would accrue to the organisation through the creation of additional leadership mechanisms for these activities.

IT, in contrast, is not as well understood at board level and there are usually no established IT governance frameworks inside organisations. Yet IT is critical, and it therefore needs a specialised and focused approach that will compensate for these weaknesses.

The IT steering committee has a number of functions, some of which (depending on the size, structure and complexity of the organisation) may be dealt with through sub-committees. It takes the lead in dealing with IT governance principles (including the decision-making hierarchy), strategy, and risk-treatment criteria. ISO/IEC 38500 is very clear in its statement that the board cannot escape its overall responsibility for IT, and therefore the board continues to have a key monitoring and oversight role across the whole of IT, particularly in respect of project governance. This monitoring component means that the board IT committee has similarities to the audit committee and, given the extent to which IT governance issues impinge on audit issues (particularly around internal control), there is some sense in having a number of members of each committee in common.

They are not, though, the same committee. In some organisations, the monitoring component of the IT governance framework will be included in the agenda of the audit committee, in order to ensure a clear segregation between those responsible for determining the ICT strategy of the organisation and approving investment, and those responsible for monitoring and overseeing the appropriateness and effectiveness of those decisions.

Composition of the IT steering committee

The composition of the IT steering committee should be straightforward. The chair should be selected on exactly the same basis as the chair of the audit committee; i.e. it should be someone with recent and relevant senior IT management experience. There should be a majority of independent directors on the committee, and key executives should be invited to attend; as a minimum the CEO, the CFO and the CIO (or equivalent) should be included. In some organisations, it would be appropriate to include the CCO as well.

Key tips for creating an effective IT steering committee include the following:

- There must be at least one independent director who has the right mix of business and IT experience and sufficient gravitas to lead the board's IT governance efforts.
- All the other non-executive directors should be mandated – and prepared and determined – to exercise informed and effective oversight of the organisation's IT strategy and its execution.
- The executive – particularly the CIO and the IT management – should be banned from using IT jargon, and forced to discuss IT in terms that are comprehensible to the non-IT specialist, with a focus on opportunities, issues, risks and plans.
- The IT steering committee should have access to external, professional advice on this as on other matters. Outside experts (strategic IT consultants) should be employed as board advisers with the specific brief of confirming that what the board has been told is accurate, complete and true and, if it is not, ascertaining what has been misrepresented or left out.

Executive IT committee

The executive is responsible for executing the board's IT strategy. Creating an executive IT committee is a common way of approaching this. The key business heads in the organisation (whether production, procurement, retail, sales, marketing, or other) might belong to the executive committee, which should be led by either the CEO or the CIO.

The CIO's position and level of accountability should be clear. He or she should be on the same level, and have the same status, as the CFO and the other functional heads (sales, marketing, etc.), with direct responsibility for managing the IT operations, and personal accountability for the success of organisational IT activity.

CHAPTER 16: ENTERPRISE IT ARCHITECTURE COMMITTEE

In *IT Governance: Guidelines for Directors*[101] we discussed the hierarchy of IT decision-making, the importance of an enterprise IT architecture, and the relationship between the enterprise architecture committee and the technology committee. This chapter looks in more detail at the role and work of the enterprise architecture committee.

Centralised or decentralised IT?

A key architectural debate that all organisations must resolve is the extent to which IT – as an infrastructure and as a functional department (or organisation) – is centralised or decentralised. The question as to whether or not IT (or parts of it) should be outsourced is entirely subsidiary to this key strategic issue, and the criteria for resolving it are different. In fact, any consideration of outsourcing options can only take place after the enterprise IT architecture decisions have been finalised.

There is no absolute answer to this question, and the right answer for one organisation is not necessarily right for another. In fact, even within the same industry sector, a strategy that has worked for one company will not necessarily work for its competitor. In this, as in everything to do with good governance, the imperative is NOT to do what everyone else has done, NOT to deploy someone

---

[101] Alan Calder, *IT Governance: Guidelines for Directors* (ITGP, 2005), available at www.itgovernance.co.uk/products/19.

else's solution, NOT to let the IT leadership determine the strategy and NOT to let false (usually political, involving control over budgets and key business infrastructure) arguments derail what should be a board-driven process.

In organisations seeking sectoral cost leadership positions, for example, or those whose primary drivers include significant cost-performance criteria, there is an obvious argument for a centralised IT infrastructure that delivers critical information, fast, from dispersed sites to central users (logistics, purchasing, sales, marketing, finance, and management) and at the lowest possible total cost of ownership.

There are other organisations whose competitive positioning is (for instance) about agility, customer responsiveness or local cultural integration, for which a decentralised IT infrastructure is more appropriate, because each division or business unit offers products and services that are sufficiently distinctive to require different technological expressions. Of course, even highly decentralised organisations are likely to have a requirement for regular reporting of specific financial and performance data in a standard format, and this information requirement has to be built into the organisation's information strategy.

The right strategic postural option – centralisation or decentralisation – is, in other words, no more than a consequence of the board's strategic business goals, competitive positioning and risk treatment decisions. The board determines and mandates the IT posture; the enterprise architecture committee works out how to deliver it. Before it is signed off by the board for deployment, the proposed enterprise IT architecture should be externally reviewed for conformance to the board's requirements by specialists who report directly to the board. This is an effective mechanism for ensuring that any deviations from the board's original requirements are openly identified and assessed; this is critical, because the enterprise IT architecture that is actually adopted will determine the organisation's business and information capabilities for a significant period of time.

Enterprise IT architecture committee

The determination of the enterprise IT architecture takes place, therefore, in the context of the business and information strategies, in line with the key IT implementation principles, and taking the organisation's security, compliance and risk treatment criteria into account. It is essential that all members of this committee have a working understanding of the board's requirements before attempting to draft the architecture documents.

The simplest way of achieving this is to set down in writing the board's requirements (strategic business goals, information strategy, IT implementation principles, and security, compliance and risk treatment criteria in relation to information and IT), circulate the document to all members of the IT architecture committee, and enable an open discussion between these members and key board members and executives (CIO, CEO, for instance), whose sole purpose is to ensure that there is commonality of understanding – both of the board requirements and of any possible adverse consequences that the technology specialists identify.

Adverse consequences should trigger a fast, reiterative process to adjust the board's strategic requirements in a way that produces a final strategy document that is capable of technological implementation.

The enterprise IT architecture itself is a set of organising principles that determine the way in which the organisation's information and communications technology will interact with its operating systems, applications and data. These architectural principles should provide the organisation with a basis for making decisions about existing IT assets as well as providing guidance on what new assets are required. The architectural principles should be sufficiently detailed to create a clearly defined, unambiguous technology framework, but should not be so granular that their level of detail impinges on individual (current or future) projects.

The architecture might, for example (if the key principles allow), need to ensure technical integration, in order to minimise inter-system hand-offs (which is where significant cost and risk reside) and allow the IT organisation to respond to business needs in a cost-effective manner. The ongoing role of this committee is to ensure that all ICT deployments (including outsourcing proposals) are in line with this requirement.

In many organisations, the enterprise IT architecture committee should be led by the CIO (or equivalent executive responsible for IT), although in complex, global organisations, the role might be delegated to a Chief Architect. The person who leads the committee should be responsible for the formalisation of the architecture and its communication across the organisation. Key members of the committee should include:

- Senior business delegates who understand the organisational architecture, and who are capable and prepared to assess architectural proposals in the light of their business needs (which ought to have been taken into account in the business and information strategies).

- Senior technical managers with expertise in systems, data, security and infrastructure.
- The organisational risk manager.

The big architectural challenge is in complex, global businesses, particularly those which span a number of business areas and which contain a number of semi-independent businesses that each make their own IT decisions. Of course, this challenge will only exist if the holding company has determined on a common IT governance framework across the group as a whole; a more normal approach would be for the holding company to mandate a number of fundamental IT governance principles that must be applied in each of the operating companies – in just the same way as it does corporate governance principles. These principles are then cascaded down to the operating entities through individual architecture committees, each structured to reflect the organisation of its own specific business unit. A senior member of whatever central IT oversight unit exists should sit on and have oversight of the activities of the business unit committees, to ensure that the corporate principles are being properly applied.

In circumstances where there are significant business benefits to be gained from extending a common architecture across a number of operating divisions/businesses, it will be essential that the individual business heads are wholly committed to an IT governance process that starts with the definition of a group strategy.

In virtually every organisation, however, any enterprise IT architecture project will have to deal with two strands of activity. The first is the top-down process of identifying what the organisation actually needs (following the decision hierarchy described in this book), and the second is assessing the state of the current infrastructure, so that it can be compared with the detail of what is required. The practitioner's challenge is then to map the route from where the organisation is today to where it wants to be tomorrow. A conceptual, overarching enterprise architecture framework can help this process enormously.

The Zachman Framework

The Zachman Framework is a widely accepted and widely used enterprise IT architectural framework, originally published in 1987 by John Zachman. The Zachman Institute for Framework Advancement (ZIFA) was created to take forward a vision whose original expression was: 'to keep the business from disintegrating, the concept of information systems architecture is becoming less of an option and more of a necessity'[102]. The Zachman Framework was designed to provide a 'blueprint' – a 'common vocabulary and a set of perspectives, a framework, for defining and describing today's complex enterprise systems'[103].

The Zachman Framework is a 6x6 matrix[104]. The six rows represent the perspectives of the:

---

[102] John Zachman, quoted on the ZIFA website, www.zifa.com.
[103] Ibid.
[104] A copy can be downloaded from:
www.zachmaninternational.com/images/stories/The%20Zachman%20Framework.pdf.

1 planner (scope: contextual, including external strategic requirements, drivers, implementation principles; including cost, etc.).
2 owner (business model: contextual, including the business processes and entities and their interactions and relationships).
3 designer (system model: logical, including the software functions and data elements in the logical system model).
4 builder (technology model: physical, including the physical models that will enable the logical model).
5 sub-contractor (component: detail, discrete components that can be committed for implementation).
6 the functioning enterprise, the working system (operations).

The six columns each deal with one of six questions:

1 What? What data and entities are involved?
2 How? What functions or processes are involved?
3 Where? What are the geographic and functional organisations that are involved in the network?
4 Who? What human relationships exist within the system?
5 When? What are the business- or event-cycles?
6 Why? What are the motivations at each level?

In this framework, the columns are independent of one another – in other words, 'data' does not have to be dealt with before 'function'. The relationships within each column are unique to that column and each cell is unique.

The rows represent levels of detail, beginning with the scope and business model levels, which deal with business goals and strategies and the models that are expected to deliver those goals. The further down the levels one moves, the more detailed the treatment becomes. The usefulness of this framework lies in the fact that it provides a logical and coherent conceptual starting point for any enterprise IT architecture committee; while a new project might be considered progressively and sequentially from the first level down to the bottom (i.e. from strategic context down to a functioning element of the infrastructure), the reality is that most organisations that are tackling IT governance for the first time will have an IT infrastructure that is not necessarily aligned with its business goals.

The Zachman Framework enables any one element to be contextualised with those to which it relates, so that the missing cells in relation to the starting point can be immediately identified and steps taken to fill them. For instance, an organisation may have deployed an information security architecture for which there is a clear physical technology model, but to which the users do not relate effectively; there is no logical, system model. The information security processes might interrupt and cut across the business processes; there is no working business model, and that, not surprisingly, is because the organisation has not formally identified the people (e.g. customers) and organisations (e.g. suppliers) that are important to it.

The Zachman Framework can be used as the common framework for assessing the current actual IT infrastructure as well as the organisation's future needs. The current infrastructure should be mapped to the cells of the framework, so that its strengths, weaknesses and missing elements can be identified. It should also be followed, separately and top down, to identify what the future technology needs of the organisation will be. This will produce two detailed schematics that can be compared in order to identify the extent to which future needs fit with current reality.

A detailed description of how to use the Zachman Framework is beyond the scope of this book; the sensible approach for an organisation looking to deploy this framework as part of its IT governance implementation programme is to hire an enterprise architect who has experience in using the framework and/or to send a number of those who will be involved in the project to a Zachman Institute seminar (details at *www.zachmaninternational.com*).

The Open Group Architecture Framework

The Zachman Framework is, inevitably, not the only recognised enterprise IT architecture. The Open Group Architecture Framework (TOGAF), now at version 8.1.1, is a toolkit designed for adaptation by users, and is based on four 'architecture domains' which are described (by Wikipedia)[105] as:

- Business (or business process) architecture, which defines the business strategy, governance, organisation, and key business processes of the organisation.
- Applications architecture, which provides a blueprint for the individual application systems to be deployed, the interactions between the application systems, and their relationships to the core business processes of the organisation.

---

[105] *http://en.wikipedia.org/wiki/TOGAF#Enterprise_Architecture_Domains.*

- Data architecture, which describes the structure of an organisation's logical and physical data assets and the associated data management resources.
- Technical (or technology) architecture, which describes the hardware, software and network infrastructure needed to support the deployment of core, mission-critical applications.

Service-oriented architecture

Service-oriented architecture (SOA) is an enterprise architecture concept that may be likened to a web services model. A service-oriented architecture is essentially a collection of services (usually the components of business processes and/or applications that have been broken down into specific services or types of functionality) that communicate with each other. This communication can involve either simple data-passing, or two or more services co-ordinating some activity. Some means of connecting services to each other – often, but not necessarily, the Web – is needed.

An SOA should:

- provide for easy communication between clients (or users) and services (any software entity that offers to carry out one or more actions for clients).
- allow services to be coupled to create new services.
- have no boundaries.

In theory, the SOA services can be reused and combined in new and different ways, giving the organisation flexibility and cost control. Some vendors even talk of organisations pursuing SOA as their IT strategy, and have prepared suites of services, tools and roadmaps 'in an attempt to make sure that SOA implementations match the needs of the business'[106].

While SOA may create substantial benefits for an organisation, it is important to note that:

- SOA is not the same as IT governance.
- SOA is not the same as an enterprise IT architecture, although it may form part of one.
- the driver for choosing any technology has to be the business strategy, the IT implementation principles and the information strategy.

Conclusion

An organisation's enterprise IT architecture is determined by its business goals and strategy. The key IT governance objective is to plan how to implement an IT infrastructure that will meet future business and information requirements in an environment that already has substantial investments in IT. Use of the Zachman or TOGAF frameworks can assist in the planning process. Service-oriented architecture may be an appropriate component of an organisation's enterprise IT architecture, but is not a substitute for an IT strategy. In larger organisations, the enterprise IT architecture is a critical component of the IT governance framework. In smaller organisations, this function might be assumed by the IT steering committee.

The enterprise IT architecture, as noted at the beginning of this chapter, is a set of organising principles that determine

---

[106] New software tools aimed at service-oriented architecture', *Computer Weekly* (www.computerweekly.com), 27 January 2005.

the way in which the organisation's information and communications technology will interact with its operating systems, applications and data. The determination of this architecture can only take place in the context of the business and information strategies, in line with the key IT implementation principles and taking the security, compliance and risk treatment criteria into account.

The ongoing role of the enterprise IT architecture committee is to ensure that all ICT deployments (including outsourcing proposals) are in line with the architecture, fiercely warding off attempts to deploy non-standard hardware or systems – unless the architecture itself is adapted, taking into account the ramifications for existing installations, future upgrades and current projects.

CHAPTER 17: IT AUDIT

Companies have become more and more dependent on technology to support financial reporting and almost all aspects of business operations, and to manage critical information assets. Continuous changes in technology and legislation create new exposures and requirements for all organisations. This emphasises the need for competence and experience in the proper evaluation of risks related to information technology, and the adequacy of an organisation's technology control structure. Information technology is fundamental both to the work of financial auditors and to the financial audit process. It is therefore essential that auditors have a thorough understanding of the risks in IT systems that are relevant to the financial reports and to carrying out, to the extent necessary, an IT audit.

However, an IT audit is not necessarily the same as a financial statements audit. An evaluation of financial internal controls may or may not take place in an IT audit. Identification of and reliance on internal controls is a unique characteristic of a financial audit. An IT audit, on the other hand, is more likely to focus on the risks that are relevant to information assets, and on assessing controls in order to reduce or mitigate these risks.

While internal audit is a fundamental component of the internal control framework, most organisations are seriously inadequate in oversight of IT. 'Oversight', in this context, means overseen by the board and must cover more than internal financial controls. Every board needs to empower either its IT committee or its audit committee to deal with IT oversight.

There needs to be an IT audit plan. Just like the financial audit plan, it needs to reflect the organisation's key risk areas. It must collect and evaluate evidence of an organisation's information systems, practices and operations, as well as reviewing regulatory compliance, information security, IT project progress and technical implementation. In the process, it could also evaluate and report on the skills and competences of the specialised IT staff employed in the organisation.

The objective of IT audit is to provide the independent directors with real, technical assurance that the IT implementation principles and the governance framework are being applied, and to identify any areas of non-conformance that need to be drawn to the attention of the board.

Qualified IT auditors should be used for this work, and they must work within the organisation's risk and IT governance framework. COBIT and ISO/IEC 27001:2005 both provide useful IT audit frameworks, but these should be adapted to the organisation's own identified risk management requirements.

CHAPTER 18: THE ITIL/COBIT/ISO27002 JOINT FRAMEWORK

Fines, reputation and brand damage and, in some circumstances, jail time for directors are outcomes that every business wants to avoid. The growing attractiveness of IT governance is due, at least in part, to the idea that a joined-up, coherent approach to the management of IT and compliance risk will bring the organisation identifiable benefits. Organisations also want to reduce the cost and disruption of multiple compliance initiatives, and to minimise the impact of their compliance activity on customer-focused business operations. Some organisations want to go further than this, and look to get positive business returns from their investment in closing information loopholes and improving the security of their information systems.

For this to be achieved, compliance must be built into business processes, rather than being dependent on costly, after-the-fact checking. In today's competitive business environment, internal control structures must meet the governance requirements of the organisation's listing jurisdiction as well as the requirements of data protection, privacy and other regulations applicable to its business sector and the geographical areas within which it operates. It must also deliver real business benefits. It must therefore operate at a meta-regulatory level.

ISO/IEC 27002:2005, ITIL and COBIT are perhaps the three most widely known and recognised best practice IT-related frameworks. The first is the international Code of Best Practice for Information Security from the

International Standards Organisation in Geneva, the second is the IT Infrastructure Library (now at Version 3), created by the UK's Office of Government Commerce (OGC) and the third is Control Objectives for Information and related Technology (now at Version 4.1), from the IT Governance Institute, in America (ITGI). While these frameworks have different objectives, all provide established, recognised and respected best practice guidance.

COBIT, now in its fourth edition, is widely adopted in North America and, increasingly, in Europe. It is a broad and principles-based framework that looks at the management of the IT organisation and is aimed at board members, managers and auditors. It identifies 34 key information technology processes, and identifies control objectives, each of which has an audit guideline. COBIT maps to the specific requirements of the recommended internal control framework for Sarbanes-Oxley compliance and underpins the recommendations of the UK's Turnbull Guidance.

The specific focus of ISO/IEC 27002:2005 is the assurance of the availability, confidentiality and integrity of an organisation's information. These principles are, as we saw in *Chapter 5: IT Regulatory Compliance*, also at the heart of all of today's information-related regulation. The standard's key controls all map to specific requirements of existing data protection legislation and, through ISO/IEC 27001:2005 (the information security management system specification standard), it is recognised as a means of complying with EU regulations on data protection and privacy. ISO27002 is risk-assessment-driven, technology-neutral and sector-agnostic.

The growth of ITIL, which is now the most widely u service management framework in the world, was driven by outsourcing and the idea that internal IT departments are service providers who have to deliver particular levels of service to meet the needs of internal business customers. ITIL practitioners do not focus on building processes that will conform with the control requirements of auditors, because their customer is the business; ITIL is business-orientated. It is about business ownership of business-orientated processes that perform reliably and consistently, and whose correct functioning is therefore fundamental to the control environment,

New Joint Framework

ISO27002, ITIL and COBIT are all part of any best practice IT approach to regulatory and corporate governance compliance, and each has a clearly identified role in the Calder-Moir Framework. The challenge, for many organisations, is to establish a co-ordinated, integrated framework that draws on all three of these standards. The recently released Joint Framework[107], put together by ITGI (the owners of COBIT) and OGC (the owners of ITIL), makes a significant contribution.

Aligning COBIT 4.1, ITILv3 and ISO27002 for Business Benefit[108], which was first published in late 2005, has been reviewed and revised to allow for revisions to the three standards. It formalises the relationships between the three

---

[107] The Joint Framework can be downloaded from: www.itgi.org and www.ogc.gov.uk..
[108] This is available as free download from the websites of ITGI (www.itgi.org), ISACA (www.isaca.org), OGC (www.ogc.gov.uk), and TSO (www.tso.co.uk).

best practice frameworks. The key components of this document are:

- The recommendation that COBIT should be used to provide 'an overall control framework based on a [generic] IT-process model', defining what should be done at the governance (high) level.
- The mapping of ITIL and ISO27002 requirements to high-level COBIT process and control objectives.
- The ISO27002 definition of *what* must be done in terms of information security controls.
- The ITIL descriptions of *how* the different aspects of service management should be handled.

The appendices provide a detailed mapping of COBIT controls to ITIL processes and to ISO27002 controls, as well as mapping ITIL processes to COBIT control objectives

Not only does this enable ITIL, COBIT and ISO27002 projects to be cross-linked and/or integrated, it also enables organisations to draw simultaneously on the strengths of each standard. It is important to note, though, that to some extent these cross-mappings are subjective; every organisation must tailor and adapt the best practice guidance to suit its own specific circumstances and to reflect its own risk assessment and risk appetite.

Benefits of using the Joint Framework

Organisations that use the Joint Framework should be able to create a single, integrated compliance approach that delivers corporate governance general control objectives, meets the regulatory requirements of data- and privacy-related regulation, and enables the organisation to prepare for external certification to ISO27001 and, possibly, ISO20000, both of which demonstrate compliance. It prepares the organisation for future/emerging regulatory requirements, and is demonstrably a coherent attempt to comply with competing regulations and to meet complex compliance requirements.

The Joint Framework should also help organisations improve business performance, because it focuses on business processes rather than controls, and builds controls into the business processes. It enables a broad-based shift from reactive to proactive IT operations as well as enabling the effective external training and qualification of staff and a standard measure of assessing skills and knowledge.

Increased standardisation can lead to reduced costs, improved efficiency and increased quality. Because the framework applies cross-company, it reduces vertical silos of expertise and practice, thus improving communication and business effectiveness. The fact that the framework can be deployed relatively quickly (because it avoids much 'trial and error' wheel reinvention) can reduce an organisation's dependence on expensive technology experts and proprietary methodologies. In fact, leading technology organisations are already starting to map their products and solutions to the recommendations of one or more of the frameworks discussed in this book.

Implementing the Joint Framework is also, at the practical level, a foundation of IT governance and, together with ISO38500, it sits at the heart of implementing the Calder-Moir Framework.

CHAPTER 19: THE IT MANAGEMENT SYSTEM OF TOMORROW

The Calder-Moir Framework describes the relationships between a multitude of frameworks and standards. Implementation of an integrated IT governance framework requires integration, at many levels, of a diversity of standards and requirements. One approach is that set out in the ITGI/OGC Joint Framework discussed in *Chapter 18: The ITIL/COBIT/ISO27002 Joint Framework*. Another is to integrate IT management system specifications.

There are a number of elements common to the ISO/IEC 27001 and ISO/IEC 20000-1 specifications. Organisations that wish to benefit from the guidance of both standards will not necessarily – for reasons of cost and complexity – wish to implement two separate and parallel management systems.

An integrated management system (IMS) is a system that identifies these common elements and then implements them into a single management framework that will satisfy the certification requirements of both ISO/IEC 20000 and ISO/IEC 27001. The IT governance practitioner will take this opportunity a step further, and will seek to integrate other management systems and link them to both ISO/IEC 38500 and COBIT 4.1, recognising that, while each deals with different aspects of the continuous IT governance framework, each also needs to be part of a single management system.

﹐99

BSI has recently published PAS 99[109], 'Specification of common management system requirements as a framework for integration', which provides guidance on integrating management systems. This guidance may be useful to anyone considering integration of more than one management system. It specifically lists the following management system standards and/or specifications that organisations may wish to manage in an integrated way:

- ISO 9001
- ISO 14001
- ISO/IEC 27001
- ISO 22000
- ISO/IEC 20000
- OHSAS 18001.

PAS 99 identifies the six common requirements found in management system standards and identified in ISO Guide 72[110]:

- Policy
- Planning
- Implementation and operation
- Performance assessment
- Improvement
- Management review.

---

[109] PAS 99 itself is available from BSI and authorised BSI resellers; note that it provides guidance, not a specification against which a third-party audit could be conducted. See www.itgovernance.co.uk/products/652.
[110] ISO Guide 72 is also available from BSI and authorised resellers.

Helpfully, these common elements are the ones that the practitioners will themselves identify when they consider integration of their management systems.

Annex B of PAS99 contains a detailed one-to-one mapping of the common requirements of the management standards, and anyone planning to implement an integrated management system should acquire a copy of PAS 99, if only for this specific guidance.

PAS 99 makes it possible for an organisation to deploy, for instance, common documentation, management and audit processes for both ISO/IEC 27001 and ISO/IEC 20000 management systems. Such an organisation needs only:

- a single management system incorporating its quality and its information security procedures.
- a single comprehensive and integrated audit process that covers all aspects of its activity.
- a standard management authorisation, approval, monitoring, review and quality improvement process that deals with all its activities irrespective of whether they fall within the scope of the information security management system, the IT service management system or, if it already exists, the quality management system.

The note to Clause 1.2 of ISO/IEC 27001 recognises this simple principle: 'If an organisation already has an operative business process management system, it is preferable in most cases to satisfy the requirements of this International Standard within this existing management system'.

The integrated management system

The integrated management system, shown in *Figure 10* below, is a schematic representation of the relationships between:

- the IT governance standard ISO/IEC 38500 within its risk-management context.
- the three central management standards (PAS 99, COBIT 4.1 and CMMI).
- the IT and other management system specifications.
- the raft of best practice specifications, particularly ITILv3 and the codes of practice attached to the two management system specifications.

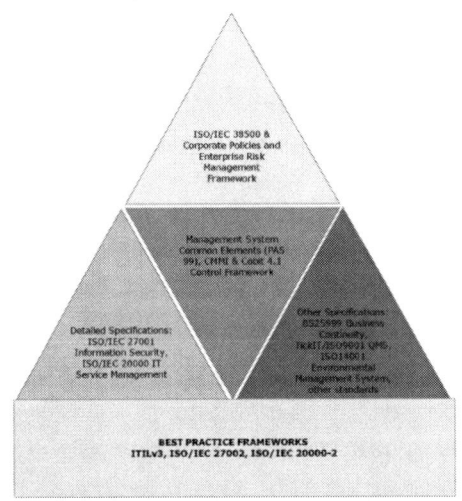

The Integrated Management System

Figure 10: The integrated management system

A single PDCA model

It is a requirement of both PAS 99 and the integrated management system that a 'process approach' will be applied to the design and deployment of the management system. This approach, widely known as the Plan-Do-Check-Act (PDCA) model, is part of the Calder-Moir Framework (see *Chapter 12: The Calder-Moir Framework*), and is familiar to quality and business managers everywhere. (It is also widely known as the Deming Cycle.) Application of the PDCA cycle to a process means that, following the basic principles of process design, there need to be both inputs to and outputs from the process. The PDCA approach should be thoroughly understood before work starts on designing and implementing the management system, and should inform every step.

ISO/IEC 27001 identifies the PDCA model in Clause 0.2 and describes how to apply it in an information security environment. ISO/IEC 27001 'adopts the PDCA process model, which is applied to structure all ISMS processes'[111].

ISO/IEC 20000 identifies the PDCA model in Clause 4, noting that 'the methodology known as "Plan-Do-Check-Act" can be applied to all processes'[112]. While the application in the IT Service Management System (ITSMS) is slightly different from that in the information security management system (ISMS), the underlying model is essentially unchanged.

---

[111] ISO/IEC 27001:2005, Clause 0.2, Process approach.
[112] ISO/IEC 20000:2005, Clause 4.

It is a requirement of both ISO/IEC 27001 and ISO/IEC 20000 that the PDCA model is applied; this requirement can be met through an integrated management system (IMS), and PAS 99 illustrates[113] how the PDCA model applies in an IMS.

The PDCA cycle, in a management system that integrates ISO/IEC 27001 and ISO/IEC 20000, has the following stages:

- Plan: establish the IMS policy, objectives, processes and procedures relevant to managing business risk in accordance with the organisational policies and objectives related to service and information security management.
- Do: implement the IMS policy, controls, processes and procedures.
- Check: monitor and measure the performance of the IMS against policy, organisational and IMS objectives and defined performance criteria.
- Act: based on inputs from the check stage, implement corrective and preventive action.

The integrated PDCA model will address both service delivery and information security management requirements by identifying and addressing requirements from various stakeholders and users of IT services and information assets of the organisation.

---

[113] PAS 99 reverses the usual order in which management system standards illustrate the PDCA cycle; it is commonly depicted as an anti-clockwise cycle.

What are the differences between the two PDCA models?

An ISMS takes as its input 'the information security requirements and expectations of the interested parties and through the necessary actions and processes produces information security outcomes that meet those requirements and expectations'[6].

An ITSMS takes, as its input, the business requirements, customer requirements, requests for new or changed services, other processes, service desk and other teams' requirements.

The principle in the integrated management system is therefore clear: the input is the specific business and customer requirements, whether these are expressed in terms of security, services or support. The management system transforms those inputs into outputs that meet the customer requirements by applying the PDCA model.

This means that the PDCA model is applied at two levels:

- At the strategic level, in terms of the overall development of the management system itself.
- At the tactical level, in terms of the development of each of the processes within the management system.

The integrated PDCA model for the IT Management System (ITMS) follows that in PAS 99. *Figure 11* over shows the LRQA[7] adaptation from figure 2 of PAS 99:

---

[6] ISO/IEC 27001:2005, Clause 0.2.
[7] See *www.lrqa.co.uk/HELP/Articles/pas99/default.aspx*.

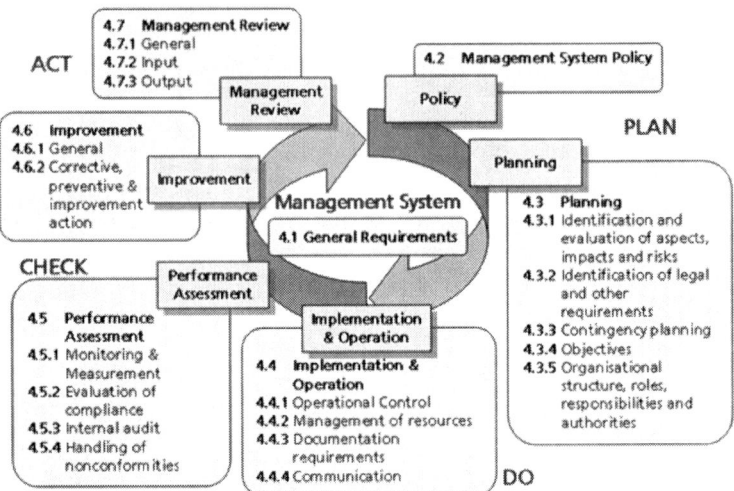

Figure 11: Integrated PDCA model for the ITMS

Aspects of integrating ISO/IEC 27001 and ISO/IEC 20000

Management commitment

The idea that management should be committed to and supportive of the implementation and continued maintenance of a management system might seem common sense, and both standards make management commitment a requirement.

Clause 5.1 of ISO/IEC 27001 (along with control A.6.1.1) requires management to demonstrate its commitment to the 'establishment, implementation, operation, monitoring, review, maintenance and improvement of the ISMS' and goes on to list the specific steps that will provide that evidence.

ISO/IEC 20000 states (in Clause 3.1) that, 'through leadership and actions, top/executive management shall provide evidence of its commitment to developing, implementing and improving its service management capability within the context of the organisation's business and customer's requirements'. This clause then goes on to specify the specific actions that top management must take.

The overlaps in these requirements enable organisations to create an integrated management process, as described by PAS 99, around a single integrated management system policy statement, underpinned with specific policies relating to information security and IT service management, and to design and implement a single method for resourcing and reviewing the design, implementation and continual review of the integrated management system.

A single documentation framework

Control A.10.1.1 of ISO/IEC 27001 explicitly requires security procedures to be documented, maintained and made available to all users who need them.

Clause 3.2 of ISO/IEC 20000 requires service providers to 'provide documents and records to ensure effective planning, operation and control of service management [including:] documented service management policies and plans; documented service level agreements; documented processes and procedures required by [the] standard and records required by [the] standard'.

An integrated management system must, in other words, be fully documented. However, not every organisation has to implement an equally complex documentation structure, and neither does it all have to be reduced to printed paper.

'The extent of the ISMS documentation can differ from one organisation to another owing to the size of the organisation and the type of its activities and the scope and complexity of the security requirements and the system being managed'[116], and 'the documentation can be in any form or type of medium'[117].

Document control requirements

Clause 4.3.2 of ISO/IEC 27001 deals with the documentation requirements for the ISMS. These requirements derive from ISO9001. Firstly, all documents need to be controlled. This means that they must:

- be approved (or reviewed and re-approved) before use.
- have a current revision and issue status (e.g. draft, final, and a version number).
- have an issue date.
- identify the document owner.
- record the change history of the document.
- be available at all points of use.
- be legible, readily identifiable and stored or used in line with their classification (see below).
- be withdrawn when obsolete.
- be appropriately identified if their origin is external to the organisation.

There are document-related controls in Annex A of ISO/IEC 27001 that would not necessarily be applied in an IT service management system but should be included in the document control aspects of the integrated management

---

[116] ISO/IEC 27001:2005 4.3.1 Note 2.
[117] ISO/IEC 20000:2005, Clause 3.2.

system. They are all important controls in their own right, and are:

- A.7.2.1 Classification guidelines, which deal with confidentiality levels, requiring that every document should be marked with its confidentiality classification.
- A.7.2.2 Information labelling and handling, which deals with showing confidentiality levels on information and information media.
- A.15.1.4 Data protection and privacy of personal information, which may affect who is entitled to see what information.

Record control requirements

Records have to be kept (as required by ISO/IEC 27001 Clause 4.3.3 and ISO/IEC 20000 Clause 3.2 d) to provide evidence that the management system conforms to the requirements of the standards. These are not the same as the records that the organisation has to keep in the ordinary course of its business, which will be subject to a variety of legislative and regulatory retention periods (and which should be specifically dealt with under ISO/IEC 27001 control A.15.1.3 Protection of organisational records).

Records that provide evidence of the effectiveness of the management system are of a different nature from those records that the ISMS exists to protect but, nevertheless, these records must themselves be controlled and must remain legible, readily identifiable and retrievable. This means that, particularly for electronic records, a means of accessing them must be retained even after hardware and software has been upgraded.

ᵤₚₑₑᵢc requirements for the creation and retention of records are identified at numerous points throughout both standards, and the documentation of the integrated management system must ensure that those requirements are met.

Electronic records and e-discovery

Any IT governance framework needs to make adequate preparation for meeting e-discovery obligations, and for ensuring that corporate records are appropriately archived and accessible throughout the retention period determined by law. E-discovery requirements vary by jurisdiction; common strands, however, include the requirements that all relevant documents be discovered, that they be readable, that they are authenticated, and that this all takes place within a restricted time frame.

BS10008 (Evidential Weight and Legal Admissibility of Evidence) and ISO15489 (Records Management) are two public standards that provide practical guidance on this subject, and organisations should look to these standards, as well as to appropriate legal advice, to ascertain what their retention obligations are and how records should be retained[118]. The combination of best practice guidance and specific legal recommendation should then be adapted into the IT management system and IT governance framework.

---

[118] See Bradley Schaufenbuel, *E-Discovery and the Federal Rules of Civil Procedure: A Pocket Guide* (ITGP, 2007), available at *www.itgovernance.co.uk/products/1000*.

Hierarchy of documentation

The approach that the organisation adopts to document approval can have a direct impact on the way in which it creates the hierarchy of documentation within its management system – and on how effectively the management system accommodates change and continuous improvement.

All documents within the management system must be approved. Approval must be by a manager with an agreed level of authority and should reflect the internal control and broader ISO/IEC 27001 requirement (A.10.1.3) for segregation of duties; the person who drafts a document should not be responsible for final approval before its release. Practically, one has to allow for revision and improvement to documents; those that are most detailed are prone to change most frequently as process improvements are identified. Given the difficulty that is usually experienced in getting senior management to find time to understand and sign off on small amendments, it makes sense for those documents that are likely to be frequently revised to be approved at the lowest possible level within the organisation.

The way to do this is to create a tiered document structure, in which those documents which undergo only infrequent change are subject to the most senior level of approval, while those likely to change frequently are subject to a much lower level of sign-off.

Policies and plans, which set general direction and requirements, should not need to change frequently, and should be subject to board (or other top management) approval. Procedures, which implement policy, are likely to change from time to time, and should be subject to middle-management approval (by the person ultimately responsible for the department or process to which the procedure applies). While neither standard specifically calls for work instructions, these can be a useful way of setting out the detailed, step-by-step requirements for carrying out specific aspects of individual procedures (e.g. as a subset of the network access control procedure, there might a work instruction that describes how the firewall server should be configured), and should be subject to approval by the person to whom the relevant asset owner reports.

We recommend an approach that uses a four-tier documentation structure, as shown in *Figure 12* over, one which is derived from the integrated management system (IMS) schematic provided earlier in this chapter.

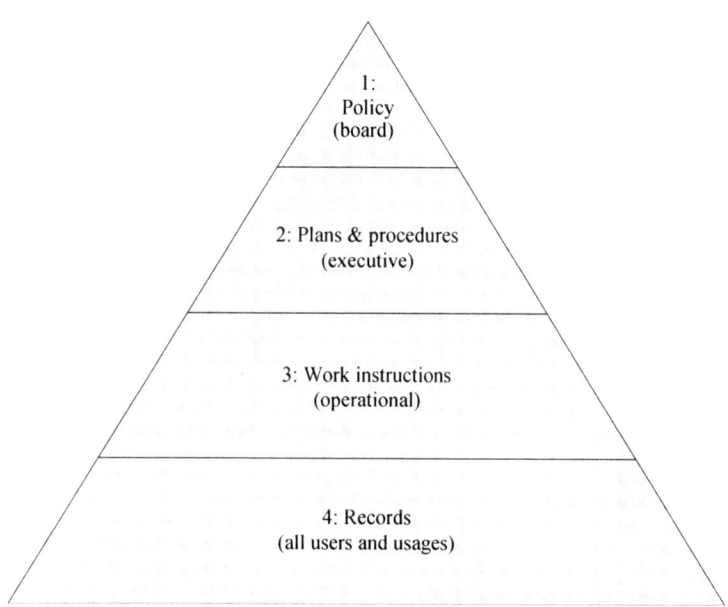

Figure 12: The four-tier documentation structure

The Policy apex coincides with the ISO/IEC 38500 apex of the IMS representation, and Plans and procedures with the various management system specifications, drawing on best practice; Work instructions and Records all underpin the best practice frameworks.

It should be noted that, within both ISO/IEC 27001 and ISO/IEC 20000, more than one 'policy' is identified. Although neither standard makes the distinction, it can be useful to think of them as being two different types of policy. The first is the overall policy that sets the organisation's general direction in respect of either information security or IT service management. The second type is a policy which sets the general direction in relation to a specific aspect of, for instance, information security, such as access control. While both policies should be approved by the board, it is worth ensuring that the second type is seen as being clearly subordinate to the first; it deals with a subset of the organisation's overall policy and its drafting should reflect that.

Single monitoring, review and audit framework

Clause 4.2.3 of ISO/IEC 27001 and Clause 4.3 of ISO/IEC 20000 both deal with monitoring and review. Both clauses strongly reflect the requirement that management be actively involved in the long-term operation and administration of the management system, while recognising the reality that the both the customer requirement and information security threat environments change quickly. This section deals, broadly, with the IMS's approach to three types of activity: monitoring, auditing and reviewing.

Monitoring

The monitoring activity required by ISO/IEC 27001 is primarily that to detect processing errors and information security events quickly so that immediate corrective action can be taken. ISO/IEC 20000 requires monitoring activity to demonstrate the ability of the IT service management processes to achieve planned results.

An organisation's monitoring activity should embrace both of these objectives. It should be formal, systematic and widespread. ISO/IEC 27001 control area A.13, Information security incident management, has at its heart the notion that the organisation must monitor for deviations and incidents, respond to them and learn from them. This principle is also fundamental to IT service management effectiveness and continual improvement.

Auditing

Audits, on the other hand, are specifically designed and planned to:

- ensure that the controls documented in the information security Statement of Applicability (SoA) are effective and being applied.
- ensure that service management requirements conform to the service management plan and the requirements of ISO/IEC 20000.
- ensure that service management requirements are effectively implemented.
- identify non-conformances and opportunities for improvement.

ISO/IEC 27001 control objective A15.2 (Compliance with security policies and standards, and technical compliance checking) deals specifically with this issue, and mandates regular, planned compliance reviews at both process and technical levels. This requirement is described in more depth in Clause 6 of ISO/IEC 27001, which lays out two important aspects of this process. The first is that the audit programme 'shall be planned, taking into consideration the status and importance of the processes and areas to be audited, as well as the results of previous audits'. The second is that 'the management responsible for the area being audited shall ensure that actions are taken without unaue delay to eliminate detected non-conformities and their causes'. These two aspects are described in the following paragraphs.

Audit programme

The audit of IT service management activities at the process level can be carried out as part of a planned series of audits that deals with all processes within the scope of the IMS, and should be integrated with the broader IT audit programme.

The audit programme plan should be risk-based, and those areas of the management system that are exposed to the highest level of risk, on which the organisation has the highest degree of dependency, or are most critical in business terms to the customer, should be audited more regularly and in greater depth than less important areas. The audit programme should also take into account changes to the customer and risk environment as well as to the management system and the business itself. Auditors should be appropriately trained and have suitable knowledge and experience, and may not audit their own work. Auditors can – and frequently are – appropriately trained employees of the company who carry out internal audit work as part of their normal day-to-day responsibilities, subject always to the requirement that they can only audit areas of activity for which neither they – nor their direct line managers – are responsible.

Management responsibilities

The management system must be clear that management at all levels of the organisation has a role to play in the effective implementation, maintenance and improvement of the system, and this should be taken into account in managerial and supervisory job descriptions, employment contracts, induction and other training, and performance reviews.

Reviewing

Reviews of internal and external audits, service management reports, performance reports, exception reports, risk assessment reports and all the associated policies and procedures are undertaken to ensure that the management system is continuing to be effective within its changing context. IT service management processes should also be measured. Finally, suitable measures must be taken to enable the organisation to baseline and benchmark its capability to manage and deliver service and service management processes.

CHAPTER 20: CALDER-MOIR IMPLEMENTATION – A 15-STEP PROCESS

Implementation of the Calder-Moir Framework follows a 15-step process, and this process draws on all the steps described in this book.

You can design and implement an IT governance framework that draws on the guidance in this book, combined with the input of an experienced IT governance practitioner, and the commitment and drive of a senior sponsoring board director. You can simplify your design and implementation process by using a toolkit such as the one available from IT Governance Ltd[119]; you will also need copies of standards[120] such as ISO/IEC 38500.

This chapter describes the 15 steps for implementing the Calder-Moir Framework. It is important to remember that the Calder-Moir Framework is a *meta-model* designed to help organisations structure their approach to IT governance; it is not a detailed and fixed compliance framework. The principles set out below are, therefore, for guidance only and their application should be liberally informed by the practitioner's and the directors' practical experience and their realistic expectations of their organisation.

---

[119] www.itgovernance.co.uk/products/519.
[120] For a full list of relevant standards, and how to obtain them, see www.itgovernance.co.uk/standards.aspx.

20: Calder-Moir Implementation – a 15-step Process

1. Initial IT governance assessment

An initial status assessment (see *Chapter 13: Implementing IT Governance*) must be performed in order to:

- establish board appetite to start governing IT.
- identify a board champion for IT governance.
- identify critical issues that IT governance will beneficially tackle.
- clarify the business case for IT governance (see *Chapter 21: Making the Business Case for IT Governance*).
- understand what IT governance activities are already in place.
- understand the organisation's (that is, the executive's and the IT management's) current decision-making hierarchy.
- understand what resources and how much commitment will be required for design and implementation of a framework.

2. IT governance road map

Develop an IT governance road map (see *Chapter 13: Implementing IT Governance*) that identifies where the organisation is and where it wants to get to. It must be communicated within the board, to the executive and to the IT organisation. The road map identifies the:

- drivers of IT governance
- objectives for IT governance
- desired end states and standards
- implementation steps and stages.

3. Principles – drawing on ISO38500

This step (see *Chapter 10: ISO/IEC 38500*) requires that you:

- adapt the ISO38500 principles to fit the organisation.
- identify and communicate simple, concrete outcomes and conformance criteria, related to the road map.
- define IT governance principles and agree the future decision-making hierarchy and committee structure.

4. Develop organisational momentum (commitment, governance mandate)

IT governance must be given:

- regular time on the board agenda, which requires commitment and understanding from a majority of the independent directors.
- executive structure and commitment, plus funding, commitment of fulltime or equivalent (FTE) resources, exposure, and visible promotion by executives (see *Chapter 14: Decision Making and the IT Organisation*).

5. Initial risk assessment

The initial risk assessment (see *Chapter 6: Information and Continuity Risk*) must:

- link the ERM risk register to IT risks.
- identify IT risks: these can be in terms of information security, compliance, projects, service delivery, or risks in the supply chain or anywhere in the IT value chain.

(NB: initial assessments can be expensive, very detailed, and can take a long time if not intelligently structured, planned and executed.)

6. Plan changes (see Chapter *13: Implementing IT Governance*)

The initial status and risk assessments should be used to:

- understand gaps and deficiencies in comparison to best practice, in the context of the organisational business objectives and risk environment.
- assess process maturity.
- establish an initial change programme:
  - this should not be tied to performance/reward systems.
  - choose priorities carefully.
  - attempt only a few changes at a time.
  - focus attention and efforts.
  - use 'light' assessments such as those in the *Calder-Moir Framework Toolkit* for quick feedback; these can be repeated relatively frequently.

7. Build on existing capabilities

It is likely that many IT governance processes and tools will be in place already:

- Use them, but adapt the outputs to align with the required IT governance framework design.
- Change and improve the existing processes and outputs rather than implementing wholly new targets, processes and outputs.

8. Business strategy

IT strategy must be aligned with business strategy (see *Chapter 13: Implementing IT Governance*). This requires considering:

- what is important to the business?
    - operational excellence?
    - change?
    - risk avoidance?
    - all three?
- operational and capital expenditure allocations (OpEx and CapEx)
- performance expectations
- priorities for change
- knowledge/IP.

Information and application strategies can then be derived from this information.

9. Risk, governance and compliance framework (see *Chapter 4: Governance and Risk Management*)

- Design the IT governance framework (see *Chapter 9*).
- Align IT processes and operations with business risk and compliance requirements regarding:
    - security
    - operational risk
    - testing
    - monitoring.
- Link COBIT, ITIL and ISO27002 frameworks (see *Chapter 18: The ITIL/COBIT/ISO27002 Joint Framework*).

- Select appropriate project governance methodology (see *Chapter 8: Project Governance*) and recruit/train practitioners.
- Align IT governance with organisational governance:
  - Link ISO38500 principles with broader board principles, processes and activities (see *Chapter 10: ISO/IEC 38500*).
  - Use PAS 99 for integrating management systems (see *Chapter 19: The IT Management System of Tomorrow*).
  - Consider the role of Six Sigma, CMMI and quality frameworks.
  - Determine internal control framework, internal reporting and metrics (see *Chapter 7: Internal Control Frameworks*).
  - Identify required external reporting.
  - Ensure compliance with internal and external standards and link up all IT audit and ERM audit activity (see *Chapter 17: IT Audit*).
  - Instigate legislation and compliance programmes.
  - Deploy Unified Compliance Framework (UCF)[121].
  - Take into account: privacy, health & safety, trading practices, industry regulations, environmental, human factors; green initiatives, accounting, HR; other ISO standards.

---

[121] See Dorian J. Cougias, Marcelo Halpern, and Rebecca Herold, *Say What You Do: Building a Framework of IT Controls, Policies, Standards, & Procedures* (Network Frontiers, 2007), available at *www.itgovernance.co.uk/products/1436*.

10. IT architecture and strategy

- Ensure that IT architecture mirrors organisational objectives and supports correctly derived IT strategy (see *Chapter 16: Enterprise IT Architecture Committee*).
- Ensure anticipated IT indicators align with required future business indicators.
- Ensure appropriate resourcing:
  - CapEx/OpEx
  - FTEs and external contractors
  - Competences, skills and training
  - Operational priorities
  - Support for business processes, such as configuration management database (CMDB), Service Desk, etc.
- Ensure that IT is aligned with IT industry trends (such as international or *de facto* standards). This includes using new technologies to improve operating costs and environmental impacts.
- Ensure that there are clear and realistic:
  - end-state (target) architectures that describe business and IT in the medium term (1 to 3 years).
  - roadmap(s) that describe project sequences and order-of-magnitude costs to achieve the end-state.
- Ensure engagement between IT architects, IT strategists, IT planners, business strategists, business designers, business planners, project managers, and practitioners.

11. Change

- Ensure that change projects are 360° (that is, they cover all business, IT and change issues).

- Use industry standard methodologies, and use them realistically (rather than following them slavishly).
- Have projects that are transparent and report the whole truth.
- Deliver the specified IT architecture and achieve the required business outcomes.
- Seek approvals for variances of what is delivered compared with what is required and specified.
- Reward outcomes instead of project metrics (time, budget).
- Celebrate when it has been earned.

12. Information and technology lifecycles

- Ensure that all applications, hardware inventories and software inventories have a lifecycle management plan from deployment to retirement.
- Ensure that there are no applications or inventory items that hinder change.
- Ensure that knowledge, including IP, has a management plan.

13. IT operations

- Ensure that IT services are designed and delivered to match and then meet business objectives (using, for instance, the ITIL Service Lifecycle).
- Monitor security and compliance and improve cost-effectiveness.
- Monitor efficiency and optimise processes.

14. Reporting

IT governance reporting should link to the ISO38500 principles and to the internal control framework and:

- be simple but not simplistic.
- summarise, with detail available for inspection as required.
- be consistent, from the IT practitioner and business through to the boardroom.
- be jargon-free, and expressed in terms of business strategies and outcomes.

15. Evolution and management of IT governance

- IT governance should evolve with the organisation: it should start small, and grow in sophistication using a maturity model
- Be aware that organisational changes (of both people and structure) will disrupt the evolution or stability of IT governance and might require a 'step back' to repair or rebuild IT governance processes or reporting.

The Calder-Moir IT Governance Framework Toolkit

This book has provided an overview of the 15 implementation steps together with some detailed information on specific topics. The guidance given here is supported by a comprehensive and detailed set of document templates, together with extensive and detailed implementation guidance, in the *IT Governance Framework*

20: Calder-Moir Implementation – a 15-step Process

Toolkit[122]. I would not try to implement an IT governance framework without using this toolkit!

---

[122] Available at *www.itgovernance.co.uk/products/519*.

CHAPTER 21: MAKING THE BUSINESS CASE FOR IT GOVERNANCE

It can be surprisingly difficult to make the business case for IT governance. While 93% of business leaders think IT is important for delivering the strategy, 62% say IT is not always on their board agenda[123].

In other words, the business case for IT governance still has to be made in each and every organisation. A starting point is the case for corporate governance as more than just a box-ticking exercise: as long ago as 1996, McKinsey and Company found that two-thirds of the companies in a survey would pay an 11% premium for the stock of a company with good governance practices[124].

More than that, 'companies whose boards engage in one or more of [the] three governance practices that signal board independence from management outperform their peers and produce higher returns for their shareholders'[125], as measured by economic value added (EVA – post-tax earnings in excess of the cost of the capital required to generate them).

Good IT governance makes even more sense. Research by Harvard Business School's Peter Weill and Jeanne Ross indicates that 'top-performing enterprises generate returns

[123] IT Governance Institute, 2008.
[124] Ned Regan in 'Entrepreneurial Companies, Strong Boards and Shareholder Value', *Corporate Board Member Magazine*, August 2002.
[125] Ira M. Millstein and Paul W. MacAvoy, 'The Active Board of Directors and Improved Performance of the Large Publicly Traded Corporation' (Yale School of Management Working Papers, 1997), available at *http://ideas.repec.org/p/ysm/somwrk/ysm75.html*.

on their investments up to 40% greater than their competitors'[126]. They go on to state that

Top-performing firms succeed where others fail by implementing effective IT governance to support their strategies.

Firms with above-average IT governance following a specific strategy...had more than 20 percent higher profits than firms with poor governance following the same strategy.[127]

The numbers are compelling but every organisation has to address its own IT governance requirements itself. The core elements of any business case for implementing IT governance have been touched on in this book and should include:

- Governance: enhancing corporate governance to increase stakeholder value.
- Risk management: bringing strategic IT risk effectively within the ERM framework.
- Corporate compliance: a unified, structured approach to compliance reduces cost and increases assurance.
- Corporate competitive advantage: leveraging intellectual assets to gain market share.
- Information security: against internal and external threats.
- Operational effectiveness: IT cost-effectively supporting and enabling the business, IT projects consistently delivering business value.
- Better returns: 20% higher profits, 40% greater return on investment.

---

[126] Peter Weill and Jeanne Ross, *IT Governance: How Top Performers Manage IT Decision Rights for Superior Results* (HBS Press, 2004).
[127] Ibid.

ITG RESOURCES

IT Governance Ltd sources, creates and delivers products and services to meet the real-world, evolving IT governance needs of today's organisations, directors, managers and practitioners.

The ITG website (*www.itgovernance.co.uk*) is the international one-stop-shop for corporate and IT governance professionals, providing a comprehensive range of information, advice, books, tools, training, consultancy and related services for the entire range of IT governance frameworks and best practice standards. This website serves customers internationally and has global shipping capabilities.

These books and tools are also available from within North America, by going to *www.itgovernanceusa.com*.

Pocket guides

For full details of the entire range of pocket guides, simply follow the links at *www.itgovernance.co.uk/publishing.aspx*.

Toolkits

ITG's unique range of toolkits includes the *IT Governance Framework Toolkit*, which contains all the tools and guidance that you will need in order to develop and implement an appropriate IT governance framework for your organisation. Full details are at *www.itgovernance.co.uk/ products/519*.

For a free paper on how to use the proprietary Calder-Moir IT Governance Framework, and for a free trial version of the toolkit, see *www.itgovernance.co.uk/calder_moir.aspx*.

Best practice reports

ITG's new range of Best Practice Reports is now at: *www.itgovernance.co.uk/best-practice-reports.aspx*. These offer you essential, pertinent, expertly researched information on an increasing number of key issues.

Training and consultancy

IT Governance also offers training and consultancy services across the entire spectrum of disciplines in the information governance arena. Details of training courses can be accessed at *www.itgovernance.co.uk/training.aspx* and descriptions of our consultancy services can be found at *www.itgovernance.co.uk/consulting.aspx*.

Why not contact us to see how we could help you and your organisation?

Newsletter

IT governance is one of the hottest topics in business today, not least because it is also the fastest-moving, so what better way to keep up than by subscribing to ITG's free monthly newsletter *Sentinel*? It provides monthly updates and resources across the whole spectrum of IT governance subject matter, including risk management, information security, ITIL and IT service management, project governance, compliance and so much more. Subscribe for your free copy at: *www.itgovernance.co.uk/newsletter.aspx*.

Lightning Source UK Ltd.
Milton Keynes UK
177379UK00001B/39/P